The Complete Guide to

Dalmatians

Vanessa Richie

LP Media Inc. Publishing
Text copyright © 2023 by LP Media Inc.

Publication Data

Vanessa Richie
The Complete Guide to Dalmatians – First edition.
Summary: "Successfully raising a Dalmatian from puppy to old age"
Provided by publisher.
ISBN: 978-1-954288-99-7
[1. The Complete Guide to Dalmatians – Non-Fiction] I. Title.

Design by Sorin Rădulescu
First paperback edition, 2023

Table of Contents

Introduction

The Dalmatian is an incredibly unique dog because there is nothing about the breed that is predictable. Looking at the tall, wiry-framed body with a large head, you expect a deep bark, only to be surprised by the higher pitch. They look pretty fragile too, with not much more meat on them than Greyhounds, yet this is one of the hardiest and hardest-working breeds in the canine family. They have obvious spots that color their full coat in a way that is more similar to zebras and their stripes than anything else in the animal world. The white coat with black spots is almost hypnotic as the dog races around enjoying itself, especially if work is involved.

With their big heart and love of interacting with their people, Dalmatians are great dogs for the right kind of family. Their high energy means that they need to be with a family who is also active. When they aren't properly exercised, they can be very destructive, and given their size, Dalmatians can reach a lot more than smaller dogs can.

Work is ingrained into their nature because one of their earliest known jobs was working with coaches, running alongside the horses to protect the wealthy citizens inside. They also accompanied firefighters from some of the earliest days of this profession. Romany travelers favored the breed as the dog often traveled with the more nomadic people. This gave the dog a very diverse range of associations, but always with a job that meant keeping up with horses and traveling miles at a time. From this early career path, the dog has a lot of genetically bred stamina that still holds true today.

The average Dalmatian stands from 19 inches to 23 inches at the shoulders. A healthy Dalmatian has clear muscles over a thin frame and some powerful hind legs. Though their bodies are reminiscent of Greyhounds, there are some notable differences, particularly in the type of muscles that they have. Since they were expected to go long distances, their muscles are more evenly spread over their bodies, giving them a very graceful gait when they move.

While they can be fantastic family dogs, many Dalmatians retain some of that protective nature from their days protecting coaches and caravans. When properly trained, they make fairly good guard dogs, although it does take quite a bit of dedicated training. They tend to be wary of strangers, but they don't have the same kind of protective wariness associated with more well-known guard dogs, like German Shepherds and Rottweilers. However, it is essential for anyone who adopts a Dalmatian to begin training as soon as the dog is old enough to retain the lessons. Since they are a more intelligent breed, training doesn't have to be difficult if you use the right approach. It's more a matter of making sure the dog is attentive and not distracted during the training sessions. This is one reason why activities like obedience training are strongly encouraged for families with a Dalmatian.

For people who love jogging, hiking, and generally being very active, this is a fantastic dog to add to the home. For most of their lives, Dalmatians will be up for long jogs, exploring wooded areas, and playing in the water. For individuals and families who love to be out and about, well-trained Dalmatians are perfect companions that help to keep experiences feeling new and fresh. If your Dalmatian doesn't seem tired enough, you can buy little packs and saddlebags to put him to work doing a bit more on your treks. You will need to carefully monitor to make sure you aren't overburdening the dog (Dalmatians ran with horses; they didn't pull the coaches). If you love biking, you can train your dog to run along beside you, ensuring that he is as tired as you are by the end of a trip out to exercise.

Dalmatians are considered to be senior dogs when they are seven years old, and their life expectancy is between 11 and 13 years. This is a normal life expectancy for a breed the size of the Dalmatian. Unfortunately, the periodic popularity of the breed has resulted in some unhealthy breeding practices, contributing to a wide range of health issues. Although the breed is not considered particularly healthy, many of their issues are not life-threatening, in large part because the breed did have a very healthy history until the 20th century.

This book is divided into four sections.

Part 1
Getting to Know the Dalmatian

This section provides basic information about the breed, including a brief history, a description of the breed's appearance, and its characteristics so that you can determine if this is the right kind of dog for you and your household.

Part 2
Adopting and the Early Days with Your Dalmatian

These chapters will help you plan for your Dalmatian's arrival and help you map out your first month with your newest family member.

Part 3
Training and Activities

In these chapters, we will help you understand the challenges you will face and provide the knowledge you will need to be successful in training your dog.

Part 4
Taking Care of Your Dalmatian

These chapters cover how to take care of your Dalmatian's health, the breed's hereditary ailments, and the canine ailments that come with age.

PART 1

Getting to Know
the Dalmatian

CHAPTER 1

Is a Dalmatian Right for You?

> ❝
>
> *A Dalmatian will thrive in a family that likes getting out and being active. Dalmatians are fantastic hiking or running partners. They have remarkable endurance and are always up for an adventure. They are an incredibly versatile breed who can excel at a variety of sports and events. They are a great fit for someone wanting to train and compete with their dog. Dalmatians have a natural inclination to be protective and will bark to announce visitors. They are incredibly sweet, loving, and snuggly. They will follow you everywhere and constantly make you laugh.*
>
> HEATHER PARSONS
> *Bedlam Acres Dalmatians*
>
> ❞

It is hard to think of any other breed that has the same kind of reputation for playfulness, athleticism, and abilities as the Dalmatian, in large part because of the way they've been portrayed in the media, but it is a well-earned reputation. While the breed was brought to prominence because of a movie, this is decidedly not a breed for all families.

This chapter will highlight traits that may help you decide whether or not this is the perfect dog for your home.

Characteristic	Description
What's Great About Dalmatians	
A dedicated and loving member of the family	This is a dog that adores everyone in the pack and will want to be around them as much as possible. They may be protective of children. They can also help tire children out so that parents can relax after a long day.
A fantastic exercise buddy	This is easily one of the best breeds for active people because they can engage in nearly every type of exercise. They can join you on jogs and bike rides (though you have to wait until they are fully mature and their bones finish growing). They are fabulous when it comes to nearly every type of exercise, so you will have options for what you want to do on any given day—and your Dalmatian will be happy with whatever you choose. As long as it is actively using its mind and body, this is a very happy dog.
A gorgeous coat that's easy to tend	If you want to have a dog that is easy to spend time with but doesn't require a lot of grooming, Dalmatians are a great choice. Unless they find a mud puddle or other mess to roll in, their coats are easy to groom and still always look dignified and elegant.
A loyal, loving companion	Dalmatians may want to be active most of the day, but if they are properly exercised and their minds given enough work to do, they will be happy to recline with you at the end of the day. Bonding with these loyal dogs is easy and often doesn't take very long.
A protector when needed	Dalmatians may not be an aggressive breed, but if they see someone with bad intentions, they will protect their people. As one of the earliest go-to dogs for hard labor, like firefighting and acting as guard dogs, they have some ingrained protective instincts. Once a Dalmatian thinks the threat is gone, it goes back to being a loving family dog.
A well-known goofball	That gorgeous coat and stunning eyes make Dalmatians look like canine gentlemen, but they are actually incredible goofballs. This trait comes from that nearly limitless energy and a desire to be close to their people.

Characteristic	Description
Why A Dalmatian May Not Be Right for You	
Not a first dog	This is a dog that has boundless energy, a high intellect, and a desire to be active. If you don't have experience with training a dog, a Dalmatian is not a good choice. They require a firm, patient, and consistent application of the rules. When you break the rules or allow something to slide, your dog is going to figure out how to get you to do that again. There are other breeds that are much easier to train for first-time dog parents.
Strong prey drive	Although they weren't bred to chase animals like a lot of other working dogs, Dalmatians still have a high prey drive, which makes them less fun for people with cats and small pets. This is because they did some work ridding homes of rats and joining people on hunts, but it is just as much because of the breed's love of being active that makes them prone to chase smaller animals.
Potential behavior issues	When they are young, Dalmatians need to be trained to keep them from jumping up on people because they grow fast, and that energy level kicks in early. They can be exuberant, rowdy, and destructive without proper training, a characteristic that is a much more serious issue with medium-sized to larger dogs. Since they tend to remain highly energetic well into adulthood, they absolutely must learn how to behave when they are young; otherwise, they can be difficult to control and may become destructive. Since they are intelligent, they are also known to be manipulative, looking for ways to get you to do what *they* want. There's no malicious intent behind this, but it does mean that you must know how to handle an intelligent dog that wants to outsmart you. A lot of exercise goes a long way, but you also have to know how to be firm and consistent with them to avoid this kind of behavior.
Daily vigorous exercise	If you don't like exercising or being active, this is not the dog for you. You should not think that you can train your dog to be a lounging dog because that just isn't in the Dalmatian's nature. There are plenty of other similarly sized dogs that would love to be lazy with you—a Dalmatian simply isn't that type of dog.

Characteristic	Description
Why A Dalmatian May Not Be Right for You	
Destructive when alone	Dalmatians do not do well when left alone for long periods of time. That high energy and intellect mean they get bored quickly, and this is often taken out on objects in your home. Even when they are well-trained, you have to make sure they don't get bored if you aren't home for hours-long stretches. Furniture (and other items) will be chewed if a Dalmatian is left alone and is bored for hours. And when those are chewed up, they can go after doorways, doors, and flooring.
Some bark – often	When a Dalmatian gets lonely or bored, barking may occur. Most of the time, they are pretty quiet, but when they get bored, some of them start to get really loud. To avoid annoying neighbors, you will either need to spend a lot of time training your dog, or you will need to make sure that your dog doesn't spend much time alone.
The shedding	That lovely coat does hide a dark secret—it is prolific when it comes to shedding. This is one of the breeds where the joke stands: there are two shedding seasons for Dalmatians, the first half of the year and the second half of the year. If you don't want to be cleaning up dog hair all the time, a Dalmatian may not be a good fit.
Numerous health issues	Sadly, this is something you have to worry about with Dalmatians today. Poor breeding practices during the 20th century have led to numerous health issues in the breed. Though most of them are not fatal, many of them are very serious and can decrease the quality of life for your dog. This is why it is critical to find a reputable breeder; they will have the right kinds of testing and breeding practices in place to greatly improve the health of their puppies.

Important Considerations

One of the reasons that people love well-established breeds is that you pretty much know what you are going to get, regardless of the age of the dog. Dalmatians are one of Europe's oldest breeds, meaning they have a very long lineage, and their health issues are well-known and documented. This will help you to plan for the different stages of the dog's life.

Socialization can help minimize some behaviors, but older dog breeds are largely set in their ways. The usual temperament of Dalmatians is good, but if your dog is untrained or unsocialized, you could be setting yourself up for failure with this breed. Here's what you can expect from your Dalmatian.

> 66
>
> *Choosing the ideal Dalmatian requires in-depth research of its physical and mental health. A reputable breeder will have performed tests and have documentation of all the Dalmatian's known hereditary problems. Around 10 percent of Dalmatians are born deaf, so testing is crucial in determining that your Dalmatian can hear in both ears. DNA testing for hyperuricosuria is vital to determine whether your Dalmatian has either high or low uric acid genes. High uric acid Dalmatians are prone to forming bladder and kidney stones and therefore require a special diet low in purines and with lots of water.*
>
> JACLYN HESLIP
> *Moen Lake Dalmatians*
>
> 99

This may seem like a lot of specific needs, but that's because the Dalmatian requires a lot of activity to be the amazing pet that people want. You want a breeder who is picky because that means they are more careful and caring of the puppies, and those puppies will have a much better foundation.

Adult Versus Puppy

The final question to ask yourself before you settle on a particular breed is whether you should get an adult or a puppy. The answer varies based on the individual or family. Probably the biggest consideration is size. You will need to regularly adjust collars and crates to accommodate a growing puppy. Adult dogs will require more monitoring when they

Photo Courtesy of Charleymae DogPhotography

are around other people and pets until you know their personality and temperament. Dalmatians are a good-natured breed, but without proper training and socialization, their size can make them more dangerous than smaller dogs, so you need to be prepared to quickly earn your new dog's respect and be very mindful of him for the first year.

> **"**
>
> *When looking for a Dalmatian, a family should decide whether a rescue or a puppy from a breeder is best suited for them at the current stage in their life. For instance, a young couple starting out and planning a family may look for a puppy to properly socialize with children, while a retired person may have the time and inclination to rescue.*
>
> JENNY POTTS
> *Seeing Spots Dalmatians of Spokane*
> **"**

Here are some considerations to help you determine which age dog is a better fit for your home.

Bringing Home an Adult Dalmatian

Photo Courtesy of Sam Welsch

As mentioned earlier, you need to be careful and consider if you can handle adopting an adult; if the dog is not properly trained, life can turn into a real struggle because of your new canine's stubbornness. Since Dalmatians are so big, they can be rough, even if they don't mean to be. You need to plan to start training from the moment you bring the dog home

Photo Courtesy of
Eryn Turner

because even if your new Dalmatian has been trained, you still have to prove you are someone who should be listened to. Essentially, you have to prove you are a worthy leader, just like you would at a new job, and that means being patient, positive, and kind, along with being firm and consistent.

If you have young children at home, you will need to watch your dog closely and make sure he has a positive reaction to kids, especially if you don't know the dog's history. You should also be careful about introducing a Dalmatian to other pets because they may have a desire to chase cats and other small pets. The intent usually isn't malicious, but that doesn't mean that they won't accidentally hurt them.

Adult dogs can give you more immediate gratification. You don't have to go through the sleepless nights that come with a new puppy. The odds are also that you aren't going to be starting from the beginning with house-training.

Additionally, adult dogs are awake during the day a lot more than puppies, and while it may take your new dog a bit longer to warm up to you, you can still bond much faster with an adult.

Finally, one of the biggest benefits of acquiring an adult dog is that it will already be its full size. There is no need to guess how big your dog will grow to be, and that makes it easier to purchase the appropriate-sized gear and supplies right from the start.

The following is a list of questions to consider when adopting an adult Dalmatian:

HELPFUL TIP
Dalmatian Club of America (DCA)

The Dalmatian Club of America (DCA) is dedicated to preserving and promoting the Dalmatian breed in the United States. Founded in 1905, the DCA serves as the official parent club for Dalmatians, recognized by the American Kennel Club (AKC). With a mission to protect and advance the breed standard, the DCA promotes responsible breeding practices, supports health research initiatives, and fosters a sense of community among Dalmatian enthusiasts. For more information about this club, visit www.dalmatianclubofamerica.org.

- **Can you properly dog-proof your home before the dog arrives?**

You can't simply bring a dog into your home, whether an adult or a puppy, and let him run around unchecked. To be sure he learns the rules of the house before he is allowed to roam freely, you will need to have a safe, dedicated space for your new dog. (Details of how to dog-proof your home are discussed in Chapter 5.) It will take a lot more to dog-proof your home with a medium to large breed because they can easily access items on top of counters, cabinets, and areas that are out of reach to most dogs.

- **Do you have pets that will be affected by a new dog?**

Dalmatians have to be trained young to coexist with other animals. If they aren't trained and socialized when they are young, it is best not to bring them around other pets. This means you will need to know the history of an adult before bringing the dog home to a house with a cat or dog. If you plan to bring home a puppy, training and socializing will need to be a top priority for the safety of your puppy and your other pets.

- **What is the dog's health history?**

A complete health record for a rescued Dalmatian may not be available, but it is likely you will find a dog that has already been spayed or neutered as well as chipped. Unless you adopt a Dalmatian with health issues, which should be disclosed by the rescue organization (if known), rescues tend to be less costly than puppies at their first visit to the vet. In other words, for the first few years, your Dalmatian's health care visits should not be too expensive.

Bringing Home a Dalmatian Puppy

> **"**
>
> *Dogs vary in personality, just like people. Each litter of puppies will have a variety of personalities, from playful to couch potatoes. It is important to allow your breeder or rescue organization to guide your choice of which dog will best fit your lifestyle and goals. Be sure to share what plans you have for your new dog and let them know everything about your family's activity level and habits. This way, you can be matched with the perfect partner. Picking out a dog based on looks alone may not result in the best long-term match.*
>
> CARLA WAYMAN
> *Spotted Way Dalmatians*
> **"**

Puppies are a major time investment, and a dog as intelligent, large, and energetic as the Dalmatian will make some aspects of raising a puppy that much harder. How much time can you devote to a puppy's care? Will you be able to deal with an excitable dog that has everything to learn and quickly becomes a puppy in a very large body?

A puppy will be a better fit if you can put in dedicated time for training and socializing before the dog becomes set in his ways. If you have other pets at home, a puppy is definitely a better choice than an adult because he is young and can be trained to follow your rules. The exception would be if you find an adult that is already well-socialized.

Photo Courtesy of
Heather Parsons

When determining whether or not a Dalmatian puppy is a good fit for your home, ask yourself:

- **How much time do you have available for training and socialization?**

  All puppies are a lot of work, starting with the moment the puppy enters your care. While the Dalmatian's temperament is predictable, how you train and socialize your puppy will affect every aspect of the dog's adult life. Training and socializing can take up a large chunk of time in the beginning, but both are essential for raising a healthy, well-mannered Dalmatian.

- **Are you able to show firmness and consistency when training?**

  From the very start, you have to establish yourself and your family as the ones in charge; your Dalmatian must understand his place in the family hierarchy. You will need to be patient and consistent with your training, no matter how frustrated you may become or how cute those puppy eyes are. All intelligent dogs have a streak of stubbornness!

- **Do you have the time, energy, and budget to puppy-proof your home?**

The preparation for your puppy's arrival begins long before he first sets foot in your house. Puppy-proofing your home is as time-consuming as childproofing your home. If you do not have the time for this, then you should consider getting an adult dog. (Details of how to puppy-proof your home are discussed in Chapter 6.)

Photo Courtesy of Amy Burdis

Photo Courtesy of Lexi Simpson

You will receive records about the puppy and the puppy's parents, which will make it easier to identify any health problems your Dalmatian might experience in the future. This makes it considerably easier to keep your puppy healthy and spot potential issues before they become major problems.

Some people find it easier to bond with puppies than with adult dogs. A young puppy may be nervous in a new home, but most adjust quickly because they are predisposed to enjoying the company of those around them.

CHAPTER 2

Dalmatian Breed History

Looking at the distinctive and gallant appearance of Dalmatians, it is easy to think they are the result of careful breeding for a certain appearance. For the most part, though, this is a dog that is a result of careful breeding for specific personality traits and capabilities, making the look of the dog a pleasant surprise.

Beyond knowing that the dog was bred to meet a range of different work needs that people had, the history of one of the oldest canine breeds in Europe is largely a mystery. They have been an integral part of European life for so long that there are many different accounts of how they came to be the loyal, loving, energetic dogs that have captured the attention of people from all around the world.

Photo Courtesy of Natasha Wagner

The Disputed History of Dalmatians

Unlike a lot of breeds, Dalmatians have been around for longer than people have kept records of dog breeding. Their physique has not changed that much over centuries either, which is one of the reasons why they are so recognizable. Their thin frame makes them look similar to many depictions and artwork across three continents, with Europe, Africa, and Asia all having some claim to being the origin of the breed. However, the dog has been closely associated with the Romanies (gypsies) for a long time, and since gypsies are a nomadic people who have largely moved around Europe, it is thought that Europe is the most likely origin for Dalmatians. Dalmatians also have a strong resemblance to the Greyhound and other sight hounds that came from Africa, although their square heads are very different from the thin faces of African sight dogs. Dalmatians have become

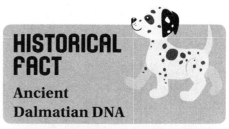

HISTORICAL FACT

Ancient Dalmatian DNA

Dalmatians have an impressive documented lineage dating back thousands of years. These stately dogs walked the palaces of ancient Egypt and graced the frescoes of ancient Greece. Scientists have recently begun to map the genomes of various dog breeds but are often stumped when it comes to Dalmatians. Though these spotted canines are most closely related to the genes of retrievers, Dalmatians are not notably similar to any of the modern retriever breeds. Many Dalmatian enthusiasts agree that the modern breed originated in 16th-century England.

so ingrained in the history of the countries across the continent that they have entered near-mythical status.

With their history in dispute, it is best to look at the details that most histories do agree on when it comes to the breed. The breed has been around for a long time, and there aren't many other breeds that have spotted coats. And none of the other spotted coat dogs are quite like the Dalmatian either. Perhaps the closest-looking breed is the Brittany Spaniel, which has a very similar build and spots. They originated in northern France during the 1800s, long after the Dalmatian had been around. English Setters have a similar height, but their build is more robust and less wiry than the Dalmatian. Great Danes have very similar frames and heads but are much larger than Dalmatians. They are also far more mellow.

Perhaps the breed with the most similarities is the German Shorthaired Pointer. They not only have a similar appearance, but they have a similar level of intelligence and energy. Both Dalmatians and

Photo Courtesy of Billy Swift

German Shorthaired Pointers have held similar jobs over their long histories, although the Dalmatian does not have the same well-honed hunting skills. However, when it comes to being active and mentally engaged, these two breeds are very similar. The spots of the shorthaired Pointer are very different from the Dalmatian's, though, so you would never confuse one of these dogs for the other.

Not Quite Like Any Other Dogs

Spots are not entirely uncommon in dogs, but they are part of a recessive gene, and dogs that have spotted coats are said to be piebald. For a dog to have a spotted coat, both parents must have the gene. The Dalmatian is the only breed that always has spots.

Many other spotted breeds have clusters and groupings of smaller spots, such as the Australian Cattle Dog and the Catahoula Leopard Dog.

This is what sets Dalmatians apart—their spots are typically large and more evenly spread out across their bodies.

They are also working dogs, but they are given jobs that few other breeds have held over the years. While most dogs have histories as hunters, herders, or helpers, Dalmatians are good at activities that other dogs likely couldn't do, such as keeping pace with horses with very little trouble.

The First Recorded History of Dalmatians

As Dalmatians are one of the most easily recognizable dogs, historians and researchers have combed through recorded history to find the dogs' first appearance. The first time people talked about this elegant-looking breed was in a small place outside of Venice, Austria, called Dalmatia, and this is where the dog got its name. For a long time, the breed was largely named based on the job it did, such as English coach dog, carriage dog, and firehouse dog. Other times, people based the dog's name on the coat, with two other names being plum pudding dog and spotted dick. Over time, people began to recognize the breed as the Dalmatian, giving the breed a unique name that matched its singular appearance. By the middle of the 1700s, the name had been widely accepted across Europe.

Photo Courtesy of Amber Miller

How the Dalmatian Got Its Spots

Unlike many breeds that have been bred to have a certain appearance, the Dalmatian's look was almost completely by accident. Given how rare piebald dogs are, it is an intriguing coincidence that their coats evolved in such a unique way.

From a practical standpoint, there is no purpose for the spots because the dog does not gain anything from having them. Given the white coat, the spots really stand out, making it a poor type of camouflage in the wild. Nor are the spots identical, with a Dalmatian's coat being like a snowflake—each coat is unique.

Photo Courtesy of
Eve Hogan

A Dog of All Trades

> **"**
>
> *Dalmatians excel at most outdoor activities. They are, of course, most notable for being a fireman's favorite breed, but they have also been used for hunting and herding and as draft and carriage dogs. They were bred to be able to run for many miles alongside carriages to protect passengers from robbers and they have great speed and endurance. Dalmatians are one of the five fastest dogs in the world and can top out at 37 miles per hour! They were also used as circus performers and love a big audience.*
>
> JACLYN HESLIP
> *Moen Lake Dalmatians*
>
> **"**

Dalmatians have a very boisterous attitude toward life. They can be great workers, but they are equally fun-loving and goofy. Their vast reserves of stamina are a direct result of their early career protecting those who were traveling, making sure their people were safe from bandits, wolves, and other threats on the road. Rottweilers have a somewhat similar build, and they protected their people going to and from the market. They were not expected to travel long distances, stopping in numerous locations like the Dalmatian. There are events where people today can watch Dalmatians participate in coaching trials, running alongside a cart or wagon and keeping up with their people. They also still have an affinity for horses that

Photo Courtesy of Casey Boyer

makes them a good companion to equines, which are known for getting spooked by other breeds of dogs.

Dalmatians were also employed to let people know that fire engines were coming through. Others would run along beside the engine to protect it from people getting too close. This is why they have largely become mascots; roads and engines have made it unnecessary for dogs to clear the way.

Their intelligence has long made them a popular part of the circus. When properly trained, it is hard to find a dog that is more willing to entertain and do tricks than the Dalmatian. They love the attention and can focus long enough to do whatever tricks their people want. They also

Photo Courtesy of
Sara Kane
KanePhotographyLLC

have an amazing ability to learn more complicated tricks and retain them over the course of their lives. If you have ever met a Dalmatian, it is pretty easy to see how such a goofy, good-natured dog would make an amazing contribution to a circus. They are natural performers with a great sense of humor. This is what can make them so wonderful as family dogs; you can train them to do nearly any trick, and your Dalmatian will love to take on the new task and keep you and your family laughing.

Photo Courtesy of Codie Schaffner

A Dog to Inspire

Dalmatians are incredibly graceful when they are in motion, whether they are running or just out for a stroll. When they are happily tired and mentally stimulated, they are quiet dogs unless there is a reason for them to make noise. They are big enough to intimidate burglars so that they don't want to break into the home.

Their look and personality are also probably what made this a breed that caught the eye of Walt Disney. The script probably seemed to write itself just by observing the breed. Once *101 Dalmatians* was released, people fell in love with the way the dogs looked and acted. The movie was a pretty accurate portrayal of how intelligent the dogs are, as well as giving people a crash course in the way the dogs go from having a milky white coat to beautiful spots over the first couple of months of the dog's life. It did give a false impression of the dog's energy levels, though. Just one is enough to keep a family on their toes.

CHAPTER 3

Dalmatian Attributes and Temperament

A Dignified Demeanor

For a lot of people, that distinctive, distinguished Dalmatian look that catches the eye is what they remember about the breed. There are a number of different standards for this breed because of how popular it has been over the last 75 years. For now, the book will focus on the standards established by the American Kennel Club (AKC).

A Trim Frame

This is a breed that straddles the line between a medium and large-sized dog, and the dogs range between 19 and 24 inches tall (to their shoulders) and between 45 and 70 pounds.

- Dogs are considered to be medium-sized when they are between 30 to 55 pounds.
- Dogs are considered to be large-sized when they are between 55 and 100 pounds (anything over that is considered to be a giant dog).

This makes the Dalmatian one of the breeds that overlaps the boundaries, making it a bit harder to plan for necessities like crates and collars because you can't be sure just how big the dog will be.

Despite not knowing exactly how tall or heavy your dog will be, the proportions are predictable. A healthy Dalmatian has a small waist and large chest. When dogs have a large chest like the Dalmatian, it means that they have large lungs so they can run.

Although they look thin, Dalmatians are muscular. One of the best ways for them to highlight just how thin and powerful they are is when they sit down in a sphinx position. Their large chests make their waists suspend over the ground while their powerful legs look like the dog is ready to spring into action at the drop of a pin. This is something that is important to keep in mind because they are food motivated. If you aren't careful, it is very easy to overfeed them since they will want you to think they haven't eaten enough. The fact that they are so active can help them to stay thin, but it doesn't mean they need a lot of extra treats or an extra meal.

FUN FACT

Spotless Puppies

Though Dalmatians are renowned for their unique spotted patterns, Dalmatian puppies are born pure white and gradually develop distinctive spots as they grow. Your Dalmatian's spots will start appearing at roughly two weeks old and may continue to develop through his first year. Though Dalmatian puppies appear entirely white at birth, the places where their spots will appear are predetermined by darker patches of skin beneath their white fur. As a result, the final spot arrangement of each Dalmatian is as unique as a human's fingerprint, and no two dogs are exactly alike.

A Regal Face

This is a breed with a very handsome face. The way their triangular ears frame their large eyes and elegant nose definitely works in the dog's favor. They can give you those puppy dog eyes to great effect if you aren't careful. They don't have particularly large jowls, so they don't have a problem with drooling (although after a long bout of exercise, they can be sloppy drinkers).

Photo Courtesy of Carrie Budzinski

They have large eyes that come in two colors, icy blue or soft brown. Sometimes they can have multicolored eyes, which is considered an issue for a Dalmatian that is intended to be a show dog. The expression in the eyes makes it clear this is an intelligent breed, and you can almost see your dog calculating what to do in response to a situation, especially if his ears are perked up.

Dalmatian ears are floppy and feel very soft. This helps them to better triangulate when there is an issue but keeps the ears from getting filled with dirt. And they make a perfect frame at the end of the longer nose, with a cute triangular tip. The tip of the Dalmatian nose may be all black, or it may be a mix of black and a lighter color.

The Famous Spotted Coat

The most unique part of the breed is its coat. When they are born, Dalmatians have a completely white coat, giving them a look like they could blend in with the snow. After 10 days, the spots start to show and will continue to get darker and larger over the next few weeks. The spots are actually set before the puppies are born; it just takes a while for the fur to grow in to match the color that the spots will be.

While people generally envision a black and white dog, Dalmatians may come in several colors. The only other acceptable spot coloring for the breed in

Photo Courtesy of Hana Sedlmayr

shows is liver-spotted. However, there is a wider range of potential colors, including the following:

- Black
- Liver
- Blue
- Brindle
- Tan
- Lemon

The base coat is always white, though.

Another aspect that people love about the Dalmatian's coat is just how easy it is to maintain. This is likely another benefit when running alongside horses and carriages. They are short-haired, with a coat that is somewhat dirt repellant. This means they don't show normal dirt easily, and grooming them is incredibly easy (at least if you tire them out before you try to make them sit still). That won't stop them from shedding, and when a Dalmatian decides to get dirty (such as playing in a puddle), it will need bathing.

A Boisterous and Bouncy Goofball

Dalmatians have a lot of love to give, and that is backed by an exuberance that seems limitless. Loyal, loving, goofy, and energetic are terms often associated with this breed. They are generally very affable and welcoming. They don't tend to have much fear, so making sure to keep them in check when you are out playing will be important, as they aren't particularly good at realizing they have limits. With their intelligence, they are able to learn to engage in games that might be a little too exuberant for a lot of other breeds.

A Real Family Dog

> 66
>
> *Dalmatians are family dogs. This breed wants to be with its people on an ongoing basis. You don't have to have a large family. Your family can be a single person. But if you do have a family of more than one person, Dalmatians will connect with everyone. Dalmatians are an active breed, which means they require regular exercise and interaction. They also like to relax. They typically adapt to their family's routine and will gauge their activity and quiet time accordingly.*
>
> LAURA FOWLER
> *Classic Dalmatians*
>
> 99

When you have a Velcro dog, you have to understand that personal space simply doesn't exist with them. This is both because they love you so much and because they don't want to miss anything. Since they want to be with you all the time, they also want to meet everyone you meet and engage in social activities with you. They may be a bit wary of strangers, depending on the situation, and sometimes Dalmatians may take a while to warm up to other people, but they tend to be more trusting with people you are comfortable around because they are attuned to the emotions of their people.

Gregarious but Protective

> **❝**
>
> *The best kind of family for a Dalmatian is an active one with space to roam. Dalmatians crave attention from their owners. They are known to be sweet and gentle to their owners, yet protective of them. Being social is one of their best characteristics, but non-socialized Dalmatians can become aggressive. They are also known to be very energetic during the day, with energy bursts. For a well-behaved Dalmatian, it is best to exercise daily.*
>
> REBECCA BIERKO
> *Georgia Dalmatians*
>
> **❞**

Dalmatians may be goofy and lovable, but their loyalty to their families means they will act if they sense someone or something is a threat. Their gregarious nature is why they aren't known as particularly good guard dogs. They are certainly intelligent enough to learn to protect people as necessary.

They are a fairly easy breed to socialize because they are prone to being happy and friendly. This means they can pretty easily slot into a home with other dogs. They will probably be fine with people and dogs outside of the home as well, but you will want to make sure they are properly socialized so they feel comfortable when you take them out.

A High-Energy Dog, High-Intelligence Breed

> **"**
>
> *Dalmatians thrive in an active family that enjoys spending lots of time out of doors. They do not like to be home alone for long periods (they get bored) and they are not dogs that do well being left outside alone or kenneled for long periods. They need lots of interaction to keep their active brain busy and lots of exercise to keep their active body busy! That said, once they get those needs met, they are happy to snuggle on the couch with you and watch TV.*
>
> SARAH GROTE, DVM
> *Willing Hearts Dalmatian Rescue*
>
> **"**

Dalmatians can be great jogging companions because they aren't prone to overheating, or they can go swimming because they are fantastic swimmers. Running alongside bikes isn't particularly difficult for

Photo Courtesy of Ashleigh Vogl

them. It may even give them enough exercise to give you an afternoon of lounging. Then, there are dog activities that can really engage them, like agility training and coursing.

The high intellect combined with the desire to please means they are generally easy to train as long as they understand they aren't the pack leaders. You can teach Dalmatians so many tricks. For example, they can learn to give hugs (something they will love because you are allowing them to invade your personal space).

The downside to the high-energy, high-intellect Dalmatian is that boredom is a constant concern. If they don't get enough exercise and adequate mental stimulation, they will come up with their own activities. This is typically going to be detrimental to your possessions, your home, and your ears. They can be prolific barkers when they are bored, even if they have been trained. From chasing animals to escaping your yard, it is too risky to leave this breed outside without supervision. Not only can they dig under your fence, but they are smart enough to figure out how to get over the top of the fence (which is usually a lot faster than digging).

Training Is Essential, Especially with Smaller Children and Dogs

> 66
>
> *Dalmatians are bright, loyal, and loving house dogs. They are strong, active athletes and wonderful partners for runners and hikers. Dalmatians can be aloof with strangers and are dependable watchdogs who protect their people. They are reserved and dignified. They are great family dogs if they are raised from puppyhood with children. It is highly recommended that a Dalmatian owner provides consistent, structured training in order to have a well-rounded, happy dog.*
>
> DEBORAH SADLER
> *Antietam Dalmatians*
>
> 99

Until a Dalmatian is fully trained and knows how to safely interact with children and smaller dogs, it is best not to have the dog around them. Dalmatians are simply unaware of their size and the potential harm they can do to smaller creatures. With smaller kids, the dog is likely to bowl them over. With smaller dogs, the Dalmatian is likely to feel that a smaller canine's desire to put some distance between them is an invitation to chase. A lot of training is essential to ensuring the safety of all parties.

Socialization is also vital, but even after being socialized, a Dalmatian may get a little too excited, in which case you need to make sure the dog will listen to you when you want him to calm down.

Playful and Enthusiastic

Properly exercised, I find Dalmatians tend to be relaxed in the house. They like to play with their toys and rough-house, but then will settle down quite nicely and hang out on the couch. Dalmatians are a fun (and sometimes challenging) combination of clever, mischievous, and athletic. It is not uncommon for me to find a Dalmatian walking around my counters. They can be trained not to get onto and into everything, but they do have a stronger tendency to be mischievous than many breeds. They are typically a very 'Velcro' breed, wanting to be with you wherever you are.

HEATHER PARSONS
Bedlam Acres Dalmatians

Photo Courtesy of Fabiola Demiraj

This is a dog that pretty much wants to play all the time. Yes, this can get a bit annoying when you want to relax, but it also means you have someone that is more than happy to help you feel better after a rough day or when you are feeling down.

If you are the kind of person who requires a bit of gentle encouragement to exercise or be more active, a Dalmatian will give you a lot of reasons to go out and experience life. They are fantastic workout partners for anything cardio-related, and they will love exploring new places with you. Their enthusiasm is contagious, and that can make even a dull run of errands feel more exciting. It's just easier to see the positive things around you when you have such an enthusiastic dog, eager to have fun with you.

Photo Courtesy of Addie Hardiman

Breed Standards

Since their history is far murkier than most other established breeds, there really isn't one right standard. If you plan to put your Dalmatian in dog shows, you will need to check the standards that apply for that show.

There are several official standards for Europe:

- Federation Cynologique Internationale
- The Kennel Club
- The United Kennel Club

In North America there are also several established standards:

- Dalmatian Club of America
- American Kennel Club
- Dalmatian Club of Canada

If you aren't sure which standards are applicable, check with whichever show you would like to enroll your dog in to make sure your dog meets the standards. For some, the color of a dog's spots will eliminate it from participation; others may disqualify a dog if it doesn't meet a particular size. This doesn't mean there's anything wrong with your dog, so you should be able to fully enjoy playing with your Dalmatian even if he doesn't become a successful show dog.

PART 2

Adopting and the Early Days with Your Dalmatian

CHAPTER 4

Finding Your Dalmatian

Though they are an old, established breed, Dalmatians are not particularly expensive to adopt, either as puppies or as adults. The initial cost for adopting a puppy tends to range between $450 and $1,200, and the initial vet visits, microchipping, and vaccinations range from $500 to over $1,200. Adults tend to cost between $50 and $500 to adopt and tend to be less costly for things like vet visits, but they will cost more for necessities like dog food and comfortable items (beds, toys, and crates).

Photo Courtesy of
Willo Carter and David Cambranes

There is a lot more to consider than just the financials, though (covered in more detail in Chapter 5). The amount of work you put into a puppy is considerably different from the kind of work you put into training an adult. An adult already has a personality and experience that may or may not make it easier to train the dog. Puppies have a predictable trajectory for training and socializing, but it can be very time intensive, especially in the early days.

To find the right Dalmatian for your home, you'll need to do a considerable amount of planning. Here are the factors to consider once you decide you want to bring home a Dalmatian.

Ways to Get a Dalmatian

> **"**
>
> *I would recommend anyone interested in a Dalmatian should do their homework. There are many wonderful breeders and also a lot of people breeding for all the wrong reasons. The Dalmatian Club of America can help in finding a reputable breeder that will guide a buyer to the right puppy for their particular needs. If rescuing a Dalmatian is what someone wants to do, there are some wonderful Dalmatian rescue groups. Once again, the Dalmatian Club of America can help.*
>
> BARBARA ALLISON
> *Rim Rock Dalmatians*
>
> **"**

This chapter is broken into two primary sections: rescuing a Dalmatian and adopting a Dalmatian. Typically, people rescue an adult, and they adopt a puppy.

- Dog rescues are one of the most reliable ways to get a healthy, adult Dalmatian. The rescuers tend to go above and beyond to ensure the health of the dog.

- Shelters are usually not dedicated to any one breed. However, that doesn't mean you can't find a Dalmatian or a dog that has a lot of Dalmatian genetics and that lovable, enthusiastic temperament.

CELEBRITY DALMATIANS

Disney Dalmatians

Dalmatians gained international fame after the rerelease of the Disney classic 101 Dalmatians in 1985. In the film, Pongo and Perdita try to keep their many puppies safe from the villain, Cruella de Ville, who hopes to make a coat from their fur. The film's rerelease caused a massive uptick in demand for these high-energy dogs, whose real-life energy levels overwhelmed many novice owners. In 2023, Dalmatians were the 49th most popular breed registered with the AKC.

While you can get puppies from both rescue organizations and shelters, it is more likely that you will find a puppy from one of the following sources:

- Breeders are the most reliable source for purebred dogs, but you have to be careful. Puppy mills focus on producing as many dogs as possible for the lowest cost. They are far less likely to do any testing and screening, so their dogs are more likely to have genetic problems.
- Pet stores may get their dogs from a puppy mill. They also aren't likely to get their dogs from great breeders. Breeders who really take care of their dogs are far more likely to be selective about who adopts their puppies.

You can find rescued puppies from puppy mills and pet stores at a dog rescue group or pet shelter. You can also get a great adult dog from a breeder, especially if a breeder takes one of their dogs back from a client who did not follow the contract. Sometimes people have to surrender their dogs, and breeders often prefer to have their dogs returned to them so they can find another good home for the dog.

To find your perfect Dalmatian, make sure to check multiple avenues unless you want a puppy, in which case a breeder is probably your best bet.

Rescuing a Dalmatian

Photo Courtesy of Alicia McClelland

Given how popular the breed is, there is almost certainly a Dalmatian within driving distance from where you live. This is a breed that tends to have a lot of specialized rescue centers around North America, so just a half hour of looking online will likely result in several rescues you can contact to see if they have an adult that might be a good fit for your family. Should you find there isn't a Dalmatian rescue group in your local area, here are a few websites that can help you find a Dalmatian or Dalmatian mix to adopt:

- Dalmatian Club of America Rescue
- Dalmatian Dog Rescue Group Directory

Between these two sites, you will likely find somewhere near you that can help you adopt an adult, regardless of where you live.

If you can't find a rescue near your home, you can also contact Dalmatian breeders to see if they have had any of their puppies returned that are at least two years old. That way, the breeders will have a better understanding of the dog and its personality, and they will be able to answer any future questions you might have. Make sure you ask the following questions when adopting a Dalmatian:

- What is the reason the dog was surrendered?
- Did the dog have any health issues when he arrived?
- Do they know how the dog was treated by the previous family? What kind of training was he given? Was he mistreated? Was he socialized?
- How many homes has the dog experienced?

- What kind of veterinary care did the dog receive? Are there records that confirm this?
- Will the dog require extra medical attention based on known or suspected problems?
- Is the dog house-trained?
- How well does the dog react to strangers while walking in unfamiliar areas?
- Does the dog tend to be aggressive or guard his food when eating?
- How does the dog react to children and to other dogs and pets?
- Does the dog have any known allergies?
- Does the dog have any known dietary restrictions?
- If there are problems with the dog after adoption, will the organization take him back?

You should always meet an adult dog before adopting and bringing the dog home. This will give you and the dog some time to get familiar with each other to see if you are a good fit for its personality.

Types of Rescues

It is possible that you will find a Dalmatian in a shelter or through a more traditional rescue group because this is, unfortunately, a breed that people often get without understanding just how active the dog is. This means it is more likely for this dog to be abandoned because people simply don't want to work with it or can't meet the dog's exercise needs. If you do find a dog through these organizations, you almost certainly will not be able to get documentation about the dog's breeding, training, and socialization. Also, the dog likely won't be well trained.

Rescue and Shelter Adoption Requirements

Adopting an adult is significantly different from adopting a puppy. Since the dogs have already been to at least one home prior to being brought into a rescue, diligent rescues want to make sure their dogs go

Photo Courtesy of
Jaclyn Heslip
Moen Lake Dalmatians

to a home that is willing and able to take care of their dogs, minimizing the likelihood that a dog will be returned. When a rescue group is dedicated to a certain breed, it will have more breed-specific methods of handling and taking care of the dogs. There are no rescue requirements or standards that apply everywhere. Some require home visits, though this tends to be fairly rare. Others have requirements for what you have to do within a set amount of time after your dog goes home with you.

In the U.S., many of the shelter requirements are based on state laws. The website NomNom has created a page that details the requirements for those living in the U.S.: https://www.nomnomnow.com/learn/article/pet-adoption-laws-by-state.

With a breed like the Dalmatian, you may have more success asking breeders if they have an adult or returned dog instead of looking for the rare rescues that specialize in Dalmatians. Many breeders require puppies or dogs to be returned to them if the adopting family is unable to continue taking care of the dog, so they may have one or two adults they are willing to adopt out. Their requirements for adopting a returned dog will be different from adopting a dog from a rescue group.

You should be able to visit the facility and meet the rescue Dalmatians. A really good rescue will want to be involved in the process and will help determine if your home is a good fit for a particular dog. Since they know the dog well, they will be pretty good judges of whether or not the dog is a good fit for your home—and this is a good sign because it means they are interested in making sure the dog doesn't need to be rehomed again.

Choosing a Dalmatian Breeder and Puppy

> *The priorities for getting a Dalmatian should be temperament, health, and what the dog is going to be used for, such as for showing or as a pet. Each of these items is equally important to sort out with yourself and the person you're considering getting a dog from. Don't under any circumstances go to a backyard breeder. Their only interest is getting your money, although they will try to convince you otherwise.*
>
> LAURA FOWLER
> *Classic Dalmatians*

If you choose to buy a dog, finding a responsible breeder is the best thing you can do for your puppy because good breeders work only with healthy Dalmatian parents, which reduces the odds of serious genetic health issues. While cost is important, it is far more important to assess the breeder to ensure you get a healthy dog.

Always take the time to do your research. Although breeders for Dalmatians are largely reputable, you might run across an individual who is more interested in making a lot of money than in caring for the dogs. The goal is to locate breeders who are willing to answer ALL of your questions patiently and thoroughly. They should show as much love for their Dalmatians as they expect you to show for your new puppy; their goal should be to locate good homes for all of their animals.

It is a particularly good sign if you find a breeder who posts pictures and information about the dog's parents, documents the progress of the mother's pregnancy, and shares descriptions of all vet visits. The best breeders will also stay in contact with you and answer any questions that might arise after you take the puppy home. Taking an active interest in what happens to the puppies in their new homes shows that breeders care a great deal about each individual dog.

Photo Courtesy of Autumn Werner

You also want to find a breeder who is willing to talk about problems that might develop with your Dalmatian. Good breeders will ensure the adopting family is capable of properly socializing and training their Dalmatians.

It is likely that your conversation with each breeder will last about an hour. Make sure you take careful notes during every interview. If a breeder does not have time to talk when you call and isn't willing to call you back—cross them off your list!

The following are some questions to consider when researching breeders:

- Ask if you can visit in person. The answer should always be yes, and if it isn't, you don't need to ask anything further. Thank the breeder and hang up. Even if the breeder is located in a different state, they should always allow you to visit their facility.
- Ask about the health tests and certifications breeders have for their puppies. (These points are detailed further in the next section, so make sure to check off the available tests and certifications with every breeder.) If they don't have all the tests and certifications, remove the breeder from your list of considerations.
- Make sure the breeder takes care of the initial health requirements, particularly shots, for each puppy from the first few weeks of birth through the dog's early months. Vaccinations and worming typically start at around six weeks of age and should be continued every three weeks. By the time your puppy is old enough to come home with you, he should be well into the first phase of these procedures or be completely finished with these important health care needs.
- Ask if the puppy is required to be spayed or neutered before reaching a certain age.
- Inquire whether or not the breeder is part of a Dalmatian organization or group.
- Ask about the first phases of your puppy's life, such as how the breeder will take care of the puppy before it goes home with you. They should be able to provide a lot of details, and they should not sound irritated by your questioning. They should also explain what training your puppy will receive prior to leaving the facility. It

is possible the breeder might start house-training your puppy. If so, ask about the puppy's progress so that you know where to pick up training once your Dalmatian reaches your home.

- Breeders should be more than happy to help guide you in doing what is best for your dog because they want their puppies to live happy, healthy lives. You should also be able to rely on any recommendations your breeder makes about taking your puppy home, particularly about the first days of living with the puppy.
- Ask how many varieties of dogs the breeder manages in one year and how many sets of parent dogs they own. Mother dogs should have some downtime between pregnancies before producing another litter. Learn about breeders' standard operations to be sure they take care of the parents and treat them as valuable family members—not strictly as a way to make money.
- Ask about aggression in the puppy's parents and find out if there are other dogs in the breeder's home. While a puppy's temperament is more malleable than an adult's, some exposure to other breeds might make it easier when integrating the puppy into a home that already has dogs. Aggression isn't a normal problem for Dalmatians, but if you have smaller animals in your home, this will be important to know.

Don't be worried about getting a little personal. Just as the breeder should have an interest in finding the right home for their puppies, you should be looking for a breeder who has a love for the breed. Here are some questions you can ask to get a better idea of a breeder's motivations.

- Why did you choose to breed Dalmatians?
- Are the sire and dam AKC champions?
- What do you look for in a new home for the puppies?

You want to have an open and transparent conversation to make sure that not only are you a good dog parent for a Dalmatian but that the breeders are a good fit for breeding and handling the puppies at their most vulnerable.

Contracts and Guarantees

> ❝
>
> *You always want to choose a Dalmatian from a reputable breeder if you don't rescue. Reputable breeders show their dogs, get all the health testing, and only breed one to two litters a year. They usually belong to a breed or all-breed club and always have a contract. You can find a reputable breeder by contacting the AKC or your local breed club, or by visiting dog shows.*
>
> DEBBIE BENNETT
> *Westview Dalmatians*
>
> ❞

Breeder contracts and guarantees are meant to protect the puppies as much as they are meant to protect you. If a breeder has a contract, make sure you read through it completely and are willing to meet all of the requirements prior to signing. Contracts tend to be fairly easy to understand and comply with, but you should be aware of all the facts before you agree to anything. Signing the contract indicates you are serious about committing to giving your puppy the best care possible and to meeting the minimum care requirements set forth by the breeder.

A contract may state the breeder will retain the puppy's original registration papers, although you will receive a copy of the papers too.

If a family does not meet all requirements as stated in the contract, it is the breeder's responsibility to remove the puppy from the family. These are the dogs some breeders offer for adoption.

A guarantee states the kind of health care the puppy is to receive once it leaves the breeder's facility. This typically includes details about the dog's current health and the recommendations for the next steps in the puppy's health care. Guarantees may also provide veterinary schedules to ensure the health care started by the breeder is continued by the new puppy parent. In the event that a major health concern surfaces, the puppy will be returned to the breeder.

The contract will also explain what is not covered by the guarantee. A guarantee tends to be quite long (sometimes longer than the contract), and you should also read it thoroughly before signing it.

Dalmatian contracts usually include a requirement that the dog be spayed or neutered once it reaches maturity (typically six months). The contract may also contain requirements for naming your puppy. If you would like more information about naming requirements, check out the American Kennel Club for details about contracts. The contract will have details of the puppy's health and a stipulation regarding what will happen if you can no longer take care of the animal. Information concerning the steps that will be taken if the new owner is negligent or abusive to the dog is also included in the contract.

Health Tests and Certifications

> "
>
> *Ensure you are aware of the Dalmatian's hearing status. All Dalmatians should be BAER (brainstem auditory evoked response) tested to ensure they can hear. If a dog is deaf, this can change its lifestyle and its daily needs. If you are purchasing a Dalmatian from a breeder, you should always ask the breeder if they have tested uric acid levels. This is also important to know, as this will determine the type of diet the dog needs, as well as determine what foods should be avoided.*
>
> FANNY FIDDLER
> *North Paw Dalmatians*
>
> "

A healthy puppy requires healthy parents and a clean genetic history, which is a bit more difficult to guarantee in a Dalmatian due to the history of this breed. A conscientious breeder keeps extensive records of each puppy and its parents. You should review each of the parents' complete histories to understand what traits your puppy is likely to inherit. Pay attention to temperament, learning traits, attachment issues, and any other personality traits you consider important. You can request these documents be sent to you electronically, or you can pick them up when you visit the breeder in person.

It might be time-consuming to review the breeder's information for each parent, but it is always well worth the time. The more you know about the parents, the better prepared you will be for your puppy.

There are a number of tests that must be run on Dalmatian parents to make sure the puppies are unlikely to have the known genetic issues associated with the breed:

- Hip evaluation (either the OFA Evaluation or the Penn HIP Evaluation)
- BAER testing to check for congenital deafness
- OFA thyroid evaluation (optional, but recommended)
- ACVO eye evaluation (optional, but recommended)

These tests do not guarantee the puppies won't have problems, but parents who score well on the tests are less likely to pass on genetic issues. Chapter 17 details the health issues that are common to the breed, their symptoms, and potential treatments.

Selecting a Puppy from a Breeder

> **"**
>
> *Pick a breeder or rescue organization that is trying to match the personality of the Dalmatian to your home. It might not look just like the dog you dreamed of, but matching your lifestyle and personality is going to bring much more happiness than just getting a dog with the right spot pattern. If buying a puppy from a breeder, meet the parent dogs before ever looking at a puppy. If you don't like the parents, keep looking.*
>
> SARAH GROTE, DVM
> *Willing Hearts Dalmatian Rescue*
> **"**

Selecting your puppy should be done in person. However, if the breeder is willing to share videos and pictures, you can start checking out your puppy immediately after he is born!

You should consider the following steps once you are allowed to visit the puppies in person:

Photo Courtesy of
Dawn Marchant

- Assess the group of puppies as a whole. If most or all of the puppies are aggressive or fearful, this is an indication of a problem with the litter or (more likely) the breeder. The following are considered red flags if they are displayed by a majority of the puppies:
  - Tucked tails
  - Shrinking away from people
  - Whimpering when people get close
  - Constant attacking of your hands or feet (beyond pouncing)
- Notice how each puppy plays with the other puppies in the litter. This is a great indicator of how your puppy will react to any pets you already have at home. If you see problems with the way one puppy plays, this could be a problem later.
- Notice which puppies greet you first and which puppies hang back to observe you from afar. This lets you know their personality and how likely they are to be laid back later.
- Puppies should not be over or underweight. A swollen stomach is generally a sign of worms or other health problems.
- Puppies should have straight, sturdy legs. Splayed legs can be a sign there is something wrong.

- Examine the puppy's ears for mites, which will cause discharge if present. The inside of the ear should be pink, not red or inflamed.
- The eyes should be clear and bright.
- Check the puppy's mouth for pink, healthy-looking gums.
- Pet the puppy to check his coat for the following:
  - Be sure the coat feels thick and full. If breeders have allowed the puppies' fur to get matted or dirty, it is an indication they are probably not taking proper care of the animals.
  - Check for fleas and mites by running your hand from the head to the tail, then check under the tail, as fleas are more likely to hide there. If mites are present, they may look like dandruff.

- Check the puppy's rump for redness and sores; try to check the puppy's last bowel movement to ensure its firmness.

Pick the puppy that exhibits the personality traits you want in your dog. If you want a forward, friendly, excitable dog, the first puppy to greet you may be the one you choose. If you want a dog that will think things through and let others get more attention, look for a puppy that sits back and observes before approaching you. That initial reaction should be on the puppy's terms as much as your own so that you can determine if the personality matches what you think will fit best in your home.

CHAPTER 5

Preparing Your Budget and Family for Your New Dalmatian

Dalmatians can get quite expensive, depending on what kinds of activities you want to enjoy with your dog. Their size means they need more food, larger equipment, and sturdier and larger toys. The budget for the first year is going to be a lot higher for a Dalmatian than for a small or medium-sized dog because that cute little puppy is going to quickly outgrow everything you purchased for his arrival. You should be prepared to adjust crates, collars, and other equipment so that they aren't too small for your growing puppy. If you get an adult, this won't be a problem—you'll just need to buy the large equipment right from the start.

Photo Courtesy of Sonia Pérez

It is estimated that a Dalmatian will cost over $20,000 over the more than a decade you have with him (around $2,000 a year). This may seem like a high cost, but when you consider that you have a dedicated workout companion, a loyal family member, and someone who loves to entertain you, it is more than worth it to trade money for the enjoyment of having a Dalmatian.

Fortunately, you don't have to pay all of that immediately. There is a high cost upfront, though, so you will want to set up a budget to help you make sure to get everything you need before your new dog comes home. The cost will vary based on the age of the dog you get. If you bring home a puppy, you will need to get several beds, collars, and other items because your puppy will grow fast. If you bring home an adult, you won't have to worry as much about getting more than one bed, collar, and similar items, but you

HELPFUL TIP

Working Dogs

Preparing your family for a Dalmatian involves understanding that this breed has a long history as a working dog; therefore, your Dalmatian will need a task to help keep him happy. Regular exercise routines and mentally stimulating activities like obedience training and interactive toys are all part of a healthy, happy Dalmatian. In addition, you can help give your Dalmatian a feeling of purpose by teaching him useful tricks or assigning him specific tasks during family outings. You can ensure a positive relationship between your family and your new dog by honoring your Dalmatian's working dog instincts.

may be spending more in the beginning to train your adult Dalmatian to make sure he understands the rules as early as possible. Puppies will be more costly in the beginning, but you will have more time with them.

Part 3 of this book goes into the details of the training and socialization of your Dalmatian. If you plan to take your dog to classes, you will need to do some research into the costs in your specific area. Make sure to include that cost in your budget. Breeders tend to strongly recommend you plan on early classes because it can help your dog learn with some distractions around him, as well as give you someone who can help you during those difficult first sessions.

This chapter will provide the details for the majority of the costs that you will need to cover to ensure you have all of the items your new pup will need before he arrives and over the first year. Since you can go online and get all of these items, the cost is predictable.

Beyond financial preparations, you will need to get your family prepared for the newest addition, especially when you are getting such an exuberant dog. Children, in particular, need to know what the rules are

*Photo Courtesy of
Theresa Ledford*

before the dog arrives. The rest of this chapter details what you need to do to prepare your family for the dog's arrival. It is a very exciting time, so before your Dalmatian arrives, you want to make sure you have all your ducks in a row.

Planning the First Year's Budget

Whether you get a puppy or an adult dog, the costs are always higher than you initially thought. Setting up a budget can help you make sure that you have as many bases covered as possible. Considering how much equipment you will need, there is good reason to start purchasing supplies a few months in advance. As you buy the items you need, you will begin to formulate an idea of how much money you will spend each month. Many of these items are one-time purchases (or won't need to be bought too often, like a bed), but many other items, like food, treats, and toys, will have to be purchased regularly.

Item	Considerations	Estimated Costs
Crate	You will need two crates—one for the puppy and one for when the puppy grows up. This should be a comfortable space where the puppy will sleep and rest.	Wire crates: $60 to $350 Portable crate: $35 to $200
Bed	You will probably need two beds—one for the puppy and one for when the pup grows up. Though you will need a second bed for your adult Dalmatian, you may want to wait until your dog is over a year old and won't grow much more so you know how big your dog will be before buying the adult bed. Since puppies grow quickly, you can get a slightly bigger bed than a puppy needs to use until he reaches his full size. This will be placed in the crate.	$10 to $55
Leash	The leash should be short in the beginning because you need to be able to keep your puppy from getting overexcited and running to the end of a long line.	Short leash: $6 to $15 Retractable: $8 to $25
Doggie bags for walks	If you walk in parks, this won't be necessary. For those who don't have daily access to free doggy bags, it is best to purchase packs to ensure you don't run out.	Singles: less than $1 each Packs: $4 to $16
Collar	You will need two collars—one for the puppy and one for an adult Dalmatian. You don't have to wait to get an adult collar since you should be able to adjust an adult collar to fit your Dalmatian regardless of his final size.	$10 to $30
Tags	These will probably be provided by your vet. Find out what information the vet provides for tags, then purchase any tags that are not provided. At a minimum, your Dalmatian should have a tag with your address on it in case the pup escapes.	Contact your vet before purchasing to see if the required rabies tags include your contact info.

The following table will help you plan your budget. Keep in mind the prices are rough estimates and may be significantly different based on your location.

Item	Considerations	Estimated Costs
Puppy food	This is going to depend on if you make your Dalmatian's food, purchase food, or both. The larger the bag, the higher the cost, but the fewer times you will need to purchase food. You will need to purchase puppy-specific food in the beginning, but that will stop after the second year. Adult dog food is more expensive, particularly for large breeds like the Dalmatian.	$9 to $90 per bag
Water and food bowls	These will need to be kept in the puppy's area. If you have other dogs, you will need separate bowls for the puppy.	$10 to $40
Toothbrush/Toothpaste	You will need to brush your dog's teeth regularly, so plan to use more than one toothbrush during the first year.	$2.50 to $14
Brush	Dalmatian coats are easy to maintain, and you should brush them regularly. When they are puppies, brushing offers a great way to bond.	$3.50 to $20
Toys	You definitely want to get your puppy toys for aggressive chewers. You will want to keep getting your Dalmatian toys as an adult (cost of adult dog toys not included).	$2.00 Packs of toys range from $10 to $20 (easier in the long run as your pup will chew through toys quickly)
Training treats	You will need these from the beginning and probably won't need to change the treats based on your dog's age; you may need to change treats to keep your dog's interest, though.	$4.50 to $15

You will need to pay attention to when items need to be replaced based on your dog's size. Ultimately, you need to establish a budget for the initial costs, then create a second budget for items that will need to be replaced. Plan to revisit this list at the end of every year for the first two years so you can make sure your dog remains comfortable and happy.

When you contact a vet to plan your first visit with your Dalmatian, request a cost estimate for the first year. The cost for shots is substantially different in a major city than in a rural area. Take the rough estimate for shots and other vet costs and add it to your budget planning for that first year. Also, put the date of the first vet visit on your calendar.

Finally, you will probably want to look up ways to clean, especially in areas where your dog eats and drinks. Dalmatians may not be particularly drooly, but after a nice round of exercise, they aren't particularly neat eaters or drinkers. Consider getting a few cloths that you can keep under the bowls to catch any mess your dog drops.

Instructing Your Children

All large dogs need the children around them to understand and abide by the rules of how to interact. This is true even with a puppy because the puppy needs to feel safe in the new home. You will need to be firm with children to make sure they don't accidentally hurt your Dalmatian or teach your new dog to be too hyperactive. As he gets bigger, your puppy can become a potential danger if he is reckless around your children.

To help your Dalmatian feel comfortable in his new home, you must make sure your children are careful and gentle with the dog, whether a puppy or an adult. Some kids may try to treat the puppy like a toy; don't let them. Take the time to make sure your children follow all of the "puppy rules" from the very beginning to ensure your puppy feels safe, happy, and isn't accidentally injured.

The following are the Five Golden Rules your children should follow from day one. They apply both to puppies and adult Dalmatians:

1. Always be gentle and respectful.
2. Do not disturb the puppy during mealtimes.
3. Chase is an outside game.

Photo Courtesy of Vanessa Wise

4. The Dalmatian should always remain firmly on the ground. Never pick him up.
5. All valuables should be kept out of the puppy's reach.

Since your kids are going to ask why these rules are necessary, the following are some explanations you can use. If necessary, modify the discussion to meet the audience—what you say to a toddler is a lot different from what you should tell a teen about playing with your Dalmatian.

Dalmatians tend to love children. You do still need to monitor younger children until you know your dog won't become too excited. Younger children may get a little too rough, and no matter how sturdy Dalmatians are, you don't want your new family member to get hurt by an overexcited child.

Always Be Gentle and Respectful

At no time should anyone be rough with a puppy. It is important to be respectful of your puppy to help him learn to also be respectful toward people and other animals.

This rule must be applied consistently every time your children play with your puppy. Be firm if you see your children getting too excited or rough. You don't want the puppy to get overly excited either because he might end up nipping or biting someone. If he does, it won't be his fault because he is still learning. Make sure your children understand the possible repercussions if they get too rough.

Mealtime

Dalmatians can be protective of their food, especially if you rescue a dog that has previously had to fend for himself. Even if you have a puppy, you don't want him to feel insecure during his mealtime because he will learn to be aggressive whenever he eats. Save yourself, your family, and your dog future problems by making sure mealtime is your dog's time alone. Teach your children their own mealtime is off-limits to the puppy as well.

No feeding your new dog from the table! From toddlers to teens, this is something you'll really need to emphasize—particularly for foods that your kids don't like. Dalmatians are pets, not garbage disposals, and no amount of cute puppy eyes should be rewarded with scraps from the table. That is a recipe for disaster, as it will get harder to convince your dog to stop begging if other people aren't following your rules.

Chase

Make sure your children understand why a game of chase may be all right outdoors (though you'll need to monitor things), but inside the house, chasing is off-limits! A three-month-old puppy is hard enough to control when he is excited and running inside the house, but a 40-pound,

Photo Courtesy of
Todd Thomas

eight-month-old puppy will be nearly impossible to manage and can do a lot of damage inside.

Running inside your home gives your Dalmatian puppy the impression your home isn't safe for him because he is being chased; it also teaches your puppy that running indoors is allowed, which can be dangerous as the dog gets older and bigger. One of the last things you want to see is your adult Dalmatian go barreling through your home—knocking into people and furniture—because he learned it was fine for him to run in the house when he was a puppy!

Paws on the Ground

It doesn't matter how adorable your Dalmatian is—he is a living, breathing creature, and he needs to have his paws on the ground (even though he will quickly grow too big to pick up). You might want to carry your new family member around or play with the pup like a baby, but you and your family will have to resist that urge. The younger your children are, the more difficult it will be for them to understand the difference. It is so tempting to treat the puppy like a baby, but this is uncomfortable and unhealthy for the puppy.

Older children will quickly learn that a puppy's nip or bite hurts a lot more than one would think. Those little teeth are quite sharp, and if a dog nips, he could accidentally be dropped—no one wants that to happen. If your children are never allowed to pick up the puppy, things will be a lot better for everyone involved. Remember, this also applies to you, so don't make things difficult by doing something you constantly tell your children not to do.

Keep Valuables Out of Reach

"

Most breeds, including Dalmatians, are very curious and are some-what fearless when it comes to climbing and adventuring around your home. All things dangerous to children are also dangerous to puppies. Unless the puppy is secure (in a crate or pen), you must supervise its every movement. They will put anything and every-thing into their mouths, so keep toys and small objects up and out of reach. It can be very expensive to remove objects from your dog's stomach or intestines.

CAROL CHASE HEALY

Fiacre Dalmatians and Parson Russell Terriers

"

Your kids will be less than happy if their personal possessions are chewed up by an inquisitive puppy, so teach them to put toys, clothes, and other valuables far out of the puppy's reach. Given how big your Dalmatian will get, you may need to get creative in how you get things out of reach. Cupboards, drawers, and other types of cabinets will probably be essential to ensuring your Dalmatian can't access things you don't want destroyed. Until they are a couple of years old, Dalmatians are far from mellow, and when left alone, destroying things will be their go-to activity when no one is around to entertain them.

Preparing Your Current Dogs and Cats

It can be a bit tricky introducing Dalmatians to a home with small animals and cats. Even puppies may want to chase those animals. To get the most well-rounded dog possible, you should start socializing him with your other dogs or pets when he is still a puppy. In most cases, this is a fairly straightforward process as long as your established pets are comfortable with you bringing a new puppy into their home. Even cats may find they can put up with your Dalmatian puppy as long as you can convince your new dog not to chase the cats. Given their history, this could prove to be a real challenge in the early days with your Dalmatian. Plan to have a safe space for your cats where your Dalmatian can't go so that your cats have somewhere they can feel safe from the exuberance of a puppy that wants nothing more than to chase them.

- The following are important tasks you should complete when preparing your current pets for the new arrival:
- Set a schedule of activities and the people who will need to participate.
- Preserve your current dog's favorite places and furniture; make sure your current dog's toys and other personal items are not in the puppy's space.
- Have playdates at your home to observe your dog(s) reactions to having an addition to the house.

Stick to a Schedule

It's essential to have a schedule. Obviously, the puppy is going to receive a lot of attention in the beginning, so you need to make a concerted effort to be sure your current pet(s) know you will still care for them. Set a specific time in your schedule when you can show your current dog(s) how much you love him (them), and make sure you don't stray from that schedule after the puppy arrives.

When you bring the puppy home, plan to have at least one adult present for each dog you have in your home. If you have a cat in the home, the introduction will need to be slow and methodical. If you bring home an adult Dalmatian, you will need to be careful and keep the dog and cat separated when you aren't around to monitor them because Dalmatians have a high prey drive. Over time, it is likely the animals will learn to be fine with each other.

Having a schedule in place for your other dogs will make it easier to follow the plan with the puppy. Once he has arrived, your puppy is going to eat, sleep, and spend most of the day and night in his assigned space. This means your puppy's space cannot block your current canine's favorite furniture, bed, or anywhere he rests during the day. None of your current dog's "stuff" should be in the puppy's area either; this includes toys. You don't want your older dog to feel as if the puppy is taking over his territory. Make sure your children also understand to never put your current dog's things in the puppy's area!

Your dog and your puppy will need to be kept apart at the beginning (even if they seem friendly) until your puppy has received all of his vaccinations. Puppies are more susceptible to illness during these early days, so wait until the puppy is protected from possible diseases before the dogs spend time together. Leaving the puppy in his puppy space will keep the dogs separated during this critical time.

Photo Courtesy of
Gemma Beastall

Helping Your Dog Prepare — Extra At-Home Playdates

The following explains strategies that will help prepare your current pooch for the arrival of your puppy:

- Consider the personality of your dog to predict what might happen when the puppy arrives. If your current dog loves other dogs, this will probably hold true when the puppy shows up. If your current dog is territorial, you will need to be cautious when introducing the two dogs, at least until the Dalmatian has become part of the pack. Excitable dogs need special attention to keep them from getting agitated when a new dog comes home. You don't want your current dog to be so excited that he makes the Dalmatian feel threatened.

- Consider the times when unfamiliar dogs have been in your home. How did your current dog react to these other furry visitors? If your canine becomes territorial, be cautious when introducing your new pup. If you have never invited another dog into your home, organize a playdate with other dogs before your Dalmatian puppy arrives. You need to know how your current furry babies will react to new dogs in the house so that you can properly prepare. Meeting a dog at home is quite different from encountering one outside the home.
- Think about your established dog's interactions with other dogs for as long as you have known him. Has your dog shown protective or possessive behavior, either with you or others? Food is one of the reasons dogs will display aggression because they don't want anyone eating what is theirs. Some dogs can be protective of people and toys too.
- If you know someone who owns a Dalmatian, organize a playdate so that your current dog becomes aware of the temperament of a Dalmatian.

These same rules apply no matter how many dogs you have. Think about their individual personalities as well as how they interact together. Similar to humans, you may find when your dogs are together, they act differently. This is something you will need to keep in mind as you plan their first introduction. (Details of how to introduce your current dog(s) and your new puppy—plus how to juggle the two new personalities—are included in Chapter 9.)

CHAPTER 6

Preparing Your Home and Schedule

The amount of time you need to spend preparing your home for a puppy versus an adult is about the same, but what you have to do is going to be very different, especially with a dog that could get to be a large dog. With a puppy, you are essentially going to need to childproof your home for toddlers. With an adult, you are going to need to kid-proof it for a large child, and you should have gates to keep your dog contained to certain areas as you figure out how he will interact with the surroundings. Doors may be enough, but you'll want gates and a dedicated area

Photo Courtesy of Sandra Bottiglieri

for both puppies and adults. This is an intelligent dog that can figure things out, so if you have doors that have handles instead of knobs (especially those that pull down), he may be able to figure out how to get out of a room with a door. For an intelligent, curious dog like the Dalmatian, you even need to childproof cabinets and areas that you wouldn't need to with a puppy, at least until your dog knows and understands the rules.

HEALTH ALERT

Deafness

Approximately 8 percent of Dalmatians are bilaterally deaf (deaf in both ears), and 22 percent are unilaterally deaf (deaf in one ear). Overall, about 30 percent of Dalmatians experience some form of deafness. Deaf dogs can lead whole and rewarding lives but require specialized care and training.

Puppy-proofing a home is nearly identical to childproofing it, but you are going to have to secure areas that are much higher up since the Dalmatian puppy is going to grow quickly. Coupled with problem-solving skills, your Dalmatian is going to be able to get into things that he really shouldn't, with food left on kitchen countertops being at a particularly high risk. Protecting your Dalmatian is the priority. You need to make sure the dog isn't able to get out of the yard or make his way into rooms that are potentially dangerous for him.

You need to complete these efforts several weeks before your dog is planned to arrive. Then you should conduct a weekly review leading up to your Dalmatian's arrival to make sure you don't miss anything and that everything is in place. You will need to check higher areas for an adult Dalmatian than for smaller dogs, especially when it comes to cords and other chewable objects that could harm your dog. Your new family member should have a safe space that includes all of the essentials. This will help to make your dog more comfortable and make the initial arrival a great experience for everyone.

Bringing a Dalmatian into the home also requires planning when it comes to your schedule. Your dog won't be able to join you for a jog for most of the first two years. So don't plan on jogging or biking with your Dalmatian for a while, but you can work around your current exercise schedule to help tire your puppy out.

As an intelligent breed, the Dalmatian has to know that you are the leader to follow and listen to, so you will need to earn your new family member's respect, which is easier with a puppy than it is with an adult (though it is easier to make exceptions for a puppy over an adult, which you should *not* do). This is why it is absolutely essential to ensure you are firm and consistent when you are training and working with your Dalmatian. When he understands you mean what you say, that will go a long way to letting him know why he should listen to you.

Creating a Safe Space for Your Adult Dog or Puppy

> **"**
>
> *Buy a lot of toys, cover the couch if you don't want it covered in dog hair, and be ready for counter surfing. Dalmatians are experts at self-service feeding and they all love furniture. If you don't want them on all the furniture, make sure you have comfortable beds in the family area. Dalmatians want to be where you are and as close as possible. Crate training is extremely helpful, but never just shove the dog in a crate and expect him to like it.*
>
> SARAH GROTE, DVM
> *Willing Hearts Dalmatian Rescue*
>
> **"**

Your new dog will need a dedicated space that includes a crate, food and water bowls, pee pads, and toys. All of these things should be in the area where the puppy will stay when you are not able to give him attention. The puppy's space should be gated so that your Dalmatian cannot get out and young children (or dogs) cannot get in. It should be a safe space where the puppy can see you going about your usual business and feel comfortable.

An adult Dalmatian will need a similar setup as a puppy, with all of the same items, but you can give the adult dog a bigger area. Pee pads may be necessary while the adult dog adjusts to the new environment, even if the dog is already house-trained.

Crates - An Absolute Essential for Dalmatians

> 66
>
> *Puppies need downtime, so I recommend a crate. If used correctly, the pup will go there when he needs a nap. A crate should never be used for punishment.*
>
> BARBARA ALLISON
> *Rim Rock Dalmatians*
>
> 99

Crate training (discussed in detail in Chapter 7) is much more likely to be difficult if you have a crate that is too big, too small, or too uncomfortable for your dog to feel like it is a safe place. To make training easier, be sure the crate and bedding are set up and ready before your dog arrives. A small, cozy space will help your dog feel comfortable while also dissuading him from using it as a restroom since he won't be able to get away from any mess he makes. If you feed your dog in the crate, he will start to associate the crate with positive things. This is a dog that can be easily swayed by food, so this is one way to help your Dalmatian think of his crate as a place he wants to be.

Never treat the crate like it is a prison for your puppy or adult dog. It's meant to be a safe haven after overstimulation or a comfortable place to go when it's time to sleep. Ensure your dog never associates the crate with punishment or negative emotions. You can also get your puppy a carrying crate in the early days to make trips to the vet easier. Both puppies and adult dogs are going to spend a good bit of time in the crate in the early days, though adults will be able to roam around your home a lot faster. At least, if the adult is already house-trained it will be a much faster process to get away from the crate.

Photo Courtesy of Lisa Bostijn

Puppy-Proof/Dog-Proof the House

The most dangerous rooms and items in your home will be as dangerous to your puppy as if he were a little baby. The biggest difference is your Dalmatian is going to become mobile much faster than a child. He will get into dangerous situations immediately if you don't eliminate all the hazards before his arrival. Be aware that puppies will try to eat virtually anything! Nothing is safe—not even your furniture—and they will also gnaw on wood and metal or clothing. Anything within reach is considered fair game! This is true for adult dogs too, but clearly, their reach will be a lot higher off the ground, including in your kitchen.

Keep this in mind as you go about dog-proofing your home. You will need to look for dangers and make sure they are removed before your Dalmatian arrives, whether he is a puppy or an adult.

Plant Dangers

Plants pose a unique risk to dogs because we are less likely to consider them than we might with a toddler or small child. Pets have a much greater tendency to try to eat plants, so you have to learn about all of the greenery around your home to make sure your Dalmatian doesn't try to supplement the food you give him with something that is potentially hazardous to his health.

Remember to check both inside and outside your home.

Mildly Toxic	Mildly to Moderately Toxic	Moderately Toxic	Moderately to Highly Toxic	Highly Toxic
Asparagus Fern	Aloe	Alocasia	Cactus	Brunfelsia
Begonia	Amaryllis	Arrowhead	Kalanchoe	Desert Rose
Ficus Benjamina	Calla Lily	Dieffenbachia		Flame Lily
Flamingo Flower	Cyclamen	Dracaena Fragrans		Kaffir Lily
Gardenia	Dracaena	English Ivy		Oleander
Geranium	Philodendron	Eucalyptus		Sago Palm
Golden Pothos		Peyote		Bird of Paradise (Strelitzia)
Jade Plant				
Schefflera				
Ti Plant				
ZZ Plant				

Indoor Hazards and Fixes

A Dalmatian will be an avid explorer, wanting to get into everything if given the opportunity, at least until he reaches a more mellow age. Get on your hands and knees to view each room from your Dalmatian's

Hazards	Fixes	Time Estimate
Kitchen		
Poisons	Keep in secure, childproof cabinets or on high shelves.	30 min.
Trash Cans	Use a lockable trash can or keep it in a secure location.	10 min.
Appliances	Make sure all cords are out of reach.	15 min.
Human Food	Keep out of reach.	Constant (Start making it a habit!)
Floors		
Slippery Surfaces	Put down rugs or special mats designed to stick to the floor.	30 min. – 1 hour
Training Area	Train your Dalmatian on nonslip surfaces.	Constant
Bathrooms		
Toilet Brush	Either have one that locks into the container or keep the brush out of reach.	5 min.
Poisons	Keep in secure, childproof cabinets or on high shelves.	15–30 min.
Toilets	Keep lids closed. Do *not* use automatic toilet-cleaning chemicals.	Constant (Start making it a habit!)
Cabinets	Keep secured with childproof locks.	15–30 min.
Laundry Room		
Clothing	Store both clean and dirty clothes off the floor and out of reach.	15–30 min.
Poisons (bleach, pods/detergent, dryer sheets, and misc. poisons)	Keep in secure, childproof cabinets or on high shelves.	15 min.

Hazards	Fixes	Time Estimate
Around the Home		
Plants	Keep off the floor.	45 min. – 1 hour
Trash Cans	Have a lockable trash can or keep it in a secure location.	10–30 min.
Electrical Cords/ Window Blind Cords	Hide cords or make sure they are out of reach; pay particular attention to entertainment and computer areas.	1–1.5 hours
Poisons	Check to make sure there aren't any poisons in reach (WD40, window/screen cleaner, carpet cleaner, air fresheners); move all poisons to a central, locked location.	1 hour
Windows	Be sure cords are out of reach in all rooms.	1–2 hours
Fireplaces	Store cleaning supplies and tools where the dog can't get into them. Cover the fireplace opening with something the dog can't knock over.	10 min.
Stairs	Cordon off so that your puppy can't go up or down the stairs; make sure to test all puppy gates for safety.	10–15 min.
Coffee Tables/ End Tables/ Nightstands	Clear of dangerous objects (e.g., scissors, sewing equipment, pens, and pencils) and all valuables.	30–45 min.

perspective prior to the dog's arrival. Even if they are a medium-to-large breed, Dalmatians are clever and can get into areas you don't think they should be able to.

If you have a cat, keep the litter box off the floor. It needs to be somewhere that your cat can easily get to it, but your Dalmatian cannot. Since this involves training your cat, it's something you should do well in advance of the dog's arrival. You don't want your cat to undergo too many significant changes all at once. The new canine in the house will be enough of a disruption! If your cat associates the change with your Dalmatian, you may find the feline refusing to use the litter box.

To get the litter box out of your dog's reach, you'll need to put it up high and preferably with several levels to allow your cat to reach it, but where it will be out of reach of your clever dog. It won't be long before your puppy will be able to get into a litter box on a cabinet, so you need to find a place accessible to cats but not to large dogs.

Finally, in case of problems, be sure your vet's number is posted on the fridge and in at least one other room in the house. Even if the number is programmed into your phone, family members or dog sitters will still need to know who to call in case of an emergency.

Outdoor Hazards and Fixes

The area outside your home also needs dog-proofing. As with the inside, you will need to check your outdoor preparations by getting down low and inspecting all areas from a puppy's perspective. Remember to

Hazards	Fixes	Time Estimate
Garage		
Poisons	Keep in secure, childproof cabinets or on high shelves (e.g., car chemicals, cleaning supplies, paint, lawn care)—this includes fertilizer.	1 hour
Trash Bins	Keep them in a secure location.	5 min.
Tools (e.g., lawn, car, hardware, power tools)	Make sure all cords are kept out of reach and never hang over the side of surfaces.	30 min. – 1 hour
Equipment (e.g., sports, fishing)	Keep out of reach, and never allow them to hang over the side of surfaces.	Constant (Start making it a habit!)
Sharp Implements	Keep out of reach, and never allow them to hang over the side of surfaces.	30 min.
Bikes	Store off the ground or in a place the Dalmatian cannot get to (to keep the pup from biting the tires).	20 min.

Hazards	Fixes	Time Estimate
Fencing (Can Be Done Concurrently)		
Breaks	Fix any breaks in the fencing. You need to make sure your Dalmatian can't easily get out of your yard.	30 min. – 1 hour
Gaps	Fill in any gaps so that your Dalmatian doesn't escape.	30 min. – 1 hour
Holes/Dips at Base	Fill in any area that can be easily crawled under.	1–2 hours
Yard		
Poisons	Don't leave any poisons in the yard.	1–2 hours
Plants	Verify that low plants aren't poisonous; fence off anything that is (such as grapevines).	45 min. – 1 hour

also post the vet's number in one of the sheltered outdoor areas in case of an emergency.

Creating a Safe, Escape-Proof Yard

> 66
>
> *I don't know that a home needs to be prepared differently for a Dal. I would suggest that a fence be installed before getting a puppy. They need room to burn off energy. A Dalmatian can and will run 100 yards in seven seconds. If he decides to take off, you will not be able to catch him. They were bred for endurance. The dog can be a mile away in no time, so a fence is your best friend.*
>
> BARBARA ALLISON
> *Rim Rock Dalmatians*
>
> 99

If you have a pool, make sure it is secure so that your dog cannot get into it without your help. Covers may not always be enough, so make sure

Photo Courtesy of
Amanda Helvey

to have fencing or some other kind of deterrent to keep your Dalmatian safe. Even if your dog loves swimming, make sure you are always around when he is in the pool. Dalmatians tend to be excellent swimmers, but that doesn't mean they know when they've hit their limits. This isn't a dog that is known for quitting after getting hurt or understanding when it is too exhausted to keep going. Dalmatians want to be engaged and active, so you have to be the one to make sure they don't overexert themselves.

Never leave your Dalmatian alone in the garage, even when the dog is an adult. Your puppy may be in the garage when you take car trips, which is why it is important to puppy-proof this area. An adult can get into even more trouble, which is pretty much inevitable when he gets bored.

Make *room* in your schedule for monthly inspections because Dalmatians may dig out of boredom or could damage a fence as a form of entertainment. This is a breed known for making crater-size holes because they don't have anything to do and you aren't around to stop them. This is also why you can never leave your Dalmatian alone outside. Always attend to your dog when he goes out to the bathroom or to play because when he is bored, he will very likely start to create ways to get out of the yard. You don't want to put your dog out to use the bathroom only to find he has escaped in the five minutes you left him outside alone.

Some dogs have even been able to break through or knock over fences because they want to hang out with the people on the other side of the fence. Even chain-link fences aren't entirely a deterrent because this is a dog that is both smart enough and athletic enough to be able to climb out. It's quite a sight to watch Dalmatians figure this out.

You actually can have a garden and a Dalmatian in the same back-yard—they are fantastic diggers, and you can encourage that to plant your garden. You will need to set up boundaries at the beginning of the project to keep the dog out of the area while you are doing the early preparations. This could be in the form of fencing or other boundaries that discourage your Dalmatian from accessing the area. Once you are ready to employ your dog's help, you can remove the boundaries.

You should create an area with shade and shelter for your dog for when you want to be outside playing during spring and summer days. You will need to make sure to use pet-friendly materials that will be friendly for your dog's paws. Avoid things like sharp stones and harsher materials,

Photo Courtesy of Bernie and Jamie Sweeney

as well as things that may be slippery. You will also want to avoid materials that retain heat so that the dog is able to lie down and cool off from playing when it is warm.

Choosing Your Veterinarian

You should choose a vet before you bring your dog home because scheduling a veterinary appointment may take a while. Unfortunately, you may not find a vet who has experience with the breed. Try to find a vet that at least has some experience with work dogs.

Every dog, regardless of age, should see a vet within the first 48 hours of its arrival home. The point is to establish your dog's baseline health. This may also be a requirement included in the contract with the breeder. Twenty-four hours is strongly recommended to make sure your dog is healthy, but this may not always be possible, which is why many places say to have it done within 48 hours. If there is a vet near you who specializes in or has worked with Dalmatians before, that will be best for your pup.

The following are some things to consider when looking for a vet:

- What is the vet's level of familiarity with Dalmatians or similar dogs, like Pointers?

It is almost guaranteed that vets in your area will not have experience with the breed, but experience with work dogs is usually helpful in learning how to treat a Dalmatian.

- How far from your home is the vet?
- You don't want the vet to be more than 30 minutes away in case of an emergency.

Photo Courtesy of
Aneta Chute

- Is the vet available for emergencies after hours, or can they recommend a vet in case of an emergency?
- Is the vet part of a local veterinary hospital, or does the vet refer patients to a local pet hospital?
- Is the vet one of several partners, or do they work alone? If the vet belongs to a partnership, can your dog see the same vet for all office visits?
- How are appointments booked?
- Can other services be performed at the clinic, such as grooming and boarding?
- Is the vet accredited?
- What is the price for the initial visit? What are the costs for routine visits that might include such things as shots?
- What tests and checks are performed during the initial visit?
- Can you visit the vet you are considering before you bring your dog home?
- If so, inspect the office environment and ask if you can speak to the vet. The vet should be willing to put you at ease and answer your questions. Even though a vet's time is valuable, they should take a few minutes to help you feel confident about your decision to trust them with your new dog's health.

CHAPTER 7

Bringing Your Dalmatian Home

Dalmatians tend to be pretty astute when it comes to sensing other people's emotions; that's why they can make good support animals. When you bring home your Dalmatian, the dog will probably pick up on the emotions you feel, although he may feel some apprehension because of the newness of the environment and situation. It's impossible to guess just how your dog will react, but you'll be able to guess how your dog is feeling with ease. Your canine will almost certainly have a sense of apprehension about a new place with all new people,

Photo Courtesy of Allison Watters

but there will also be a sense of excitement for something new. By working to make it a happy, enjoyable, and safe experience, you can make a great first impression on your newest family member.

Although this is a breed that is prone to being quite friendly, new situations are going to be scary. That's why you want to make your Dalmatian as comfortable as possible to let him know that your home is a safe environment. This chapter covers how to introduce your new Dalmatian to your home in a way that establishes a sense of safety so that he can settle in quicker. If you already have a dog, refer to Chapter 8 because you will need to introduce the animals outside of the home before your pup makes his grand entrance. Once you understand how to introduce dogs to each other, come back to this chapter to learn how to introduce your new family member to your home and any family members who weren't able to make the initial meet and greet.

If you don't have dogs, read ahead to see what to expect and how to make the experience more enjoyable for your Dalmatian.

HELPFUL TIP

Family Dogs

Dalmatians are lovely family dogs, loyal to their families, and good with children. However, while Dalmatians are friendly and outgoing, their high energy levels may be inappropriate for small children. Some experts caution against adopting a Dalmatian if your children are under six because these muscular dogs can knock small children down. Nevertheless, Dalmatians can become cherished family members with adequate socialization, exercise, and training.

Final Preparations and Planning

If you are bringing home a puppy, there are good odds that there will be a lot of anxiety and nervousness on his part. Adult dogs are less likely to feel this way unless they were at their previous home long enough to get comfortable (this is usually not the case at shelters or similar rescues), but they will still feel some level of anxiety and be wary in their new surroundings.

You can try to minimize the negative emotions, starting with taking time off from work during the first 24 to 48 hours after your dog comes home; the best-case scenario would have you at home for the first week or two. The more time you dedicate to helping your new friend become accustomed to his surroundings, the better. It's similar to taking time off when you bring home a baby. The focus is on bonding and establishing a good relationship with your dog.

Photo Courtesy of Natasha Wagner

Ensure You Have Food and Other Supplies on Hand

The day before your Dalmatian arrives, review the list in Chapter 5 and do a quick check to ensure you have everything you need. Take a few moments to consider if there is anything you are missing. This will keep you from having to rush out for additional supplies after the arrival of your new family member.

If you plan to make your dog's food, make sure you have the supplies and extra time in your schedule. Keep it all in one place so that you don't have to spend time hunting for the supplies when it's time for your Dalmatian to eat.

Make sure everything is in place before that bundle of energy reaches your door.

Design a Tentative Puppy Schedule

> 66
>
> *Routines are important. A pup will learn best when things are done around the same time each day. Feeding, potty breaks, crate time, and bedtime should become a routine for the Dalmatian to make the dog feel comfortable and know what to expect.*
>
> JENNY POTTS
> *Seeing Spots Dalmatians of Spokane*
> 99

Dalmatians require a firm hand to keep them from misusing all their energy, and a schedule can establish that you are the one dictating how things will go while giving them something to learn. It won't take long before your Dalmatian starts to put together when to expect a meal or trip outside. They are a very intelligent breed, so once they put this together (perhaps with a treat or a bit of extra playtime after they potty), they will be taking you to the door after they finish eating. You will need

Photo Courtesy of Athziri Mora

to be consistent in the beginning, but it will get increasingly easy to do since your dog will be more than happy to remind you of the schedule once he learns it.

Prepare a tentative schedule to help you get started over the course of the first week. Your days are about to get remarkably busy, so you need somewhere to begin before your puppy arrives. As you settle into a routine, you can update the schedule. Consider it a guideline so that you don't forget important tasks, especially taking your dog out for regular restroom breaks.

The following are three key areas to establish in the schedule before your puppy arrives:

- Feeding
- Training (including house-training)
- Playing

When you bring home a puppy, you may be expecting a ball of high energy. However, puppies of any breed (no matter how active they will be later) sleep between 18 and 20 hours per day. Having a predictable sleep schedule will help your puppy grow up to be healthier. Plan eating times, bathroom breaks, and playtime around your puppy's sleep schedule.

In the beginning, you won't need to worry about making sure that your puppy is tired out by the end of the day. Your puppy's schedule will revolve around sleeping and eating, with some walking and socialization time. His stamina will build fairly quickly, though; by the end of the first year, your pup will be a lot more active! As your pup starts to sleep less and play more, he will need 30 to 60 minutes of daily physical activity.

Every puppy is different, even within a single breed, so adjust the schedule based on the changes you see with your dog.

Keep in mind this is a dog that was born and bred for running alongside horses, and that is a very structured activity. The best way to ensure your dog starts to feel comfortable and understands what to expect is to give him a predictable life.

The next few sections will demonstrate why it is critical in the early days to establish a schedule; all puppies need a schedule, but with an intelligent, high-energy dog like the Dalmatian, a schedule can save your sanity in those early days.

Do a Quick Final Puppy-Readiness Inspection Before the Puppy Arrives

No matter how busy you are or how carefully you follow the puppy-proofing checklist, the day before your puppy arrives, be sure to set aside an hour or two to double-check that everything is in place. By giving your home one final review before your dog arrives, you still have time to make last-minute changes or fixes.

Initial Meeting

Review the rules in Chapter 5 with all family members on the day of the dog's arrival and before the pup actually arrives. Place heavy emphasis on how to handle the Dalmatian, particularly the part about not picking up your newest family member. The puppy is already going to be in a state of shock, so don't compound that by literally taking the world out from under your Dalmatian's feet. Reinforce the rules with your

Photo Courtesy of Heiarii Robson Snyder

children before the puppy arrives. Your children will be excited, perhaps as much as your new dog. From the first day, your children need to be on their best behavior so that your dog feels safe. Remember, following the rules goes both ways between your dog and your children.

Keep in mind that Dalmatians tend to be wary of strangers. Everyone needs to be aware to let the dog start interactions; people should not be screaming, squealing, or being otherwise very noisy, as this can be a source of anxiety for the Dalmatian. Also, people should not crowd around the puppy.

Determine who is going to be responsible for the primary puppy care and for primary training. To teach younger children responsibility, a parent can pair with a child to manage the puppy's care. The child can be responsible for feeding the puppy and keeping the water bowl filled. Of course, a parent should oversee these tasks.

Picking up Your Puppy or Dog and the Ride Home

Photo Courtesy of Treona Lovelady

A good bit of planning and preparation goes into picking up your puppy, especially if you are going to the breeder's home. If possible, do this on a weekend or during a holiday season. This will allow you unrushed quality time at home with your new puppy.

As tempting as it is to cuddle the puppy in your lap, it is safer and more comfortable for the puppy if you use a crate for the ride home; two adults should also be present for the ride. This is the time to start teaching your puppy that car trips are enjoyable. This means making sure that the crate is securely anchored; you don't want the crate to slide around while the puppy is helplessly sitting inside it.

Photo Courtesy of
Kelcee Shepherd

- The crate should be anchored in the car for safety and should include a cushion. If you have a long trip, bring food and water for the puppy, and plan to stop at regular intervals. Do not put food and water in the crate; sloshing water can scare your puppy. You can cover the bottom of the crate with a towel or pee pad in case of accidents.

- Call the breeder before you start the trip to make sure everything is still on schedule.

- Arrange for the mother dog to leave her scent on a blanket to help make the puppy's transition more comfortable.

- Make sure the second adult who will be traveling with you (highly recommended) will be on time so that the two of you can head to the pick-up destination.

- If you have other dogs, make sure all of the adults involved in the introduction process know what to do. They should know the time and place for that first neutral territory meeting.

If you do not have other dogs, you can pick up your puppy and head straight home. If you have a trip that lasts more than a couple of hours, stop periodically so your puppy can stretch, exercise, drink, and use the bathroom. Keep your puppy away from other dogs until he has gotten all of his shots; you don't want him to be exposed to a dog that is carrying a disease that your puppy is not fully protected against.

At no point should your puppy be left alone in the car. If you have to use the restroom, either go before leaving the breeder's place, or if you have a long drive ahead of you, have at least one adult remain with the puppy during each stop.

If the puppy has never ridden in a car before, someone should give him attention while the other person drives. The puppy should be in the crate, but someone can still provide comfort. The puppy will definitely be scared without his mom, siblings, or familiar people to console him. Having someone talk to the puppy will make it less of an ordeal for the little one.

When you arrive home, immediately take the puppy outside to use the bathroom. Even if he had an accident in his crate, this is the time to start training your new family member on where to use the bathroom.

The First Vet Visit and What to Expect

The first vet visit will establish a baseline for the puppy's health. This will also allow the vet to track your puppy's progress and monitor his health as he grows. In addition to providing a chance to ask questions and get advice, this initial assessment will give you more information about your puppy. It also creates an important rapport between your Dalmatian and the vet.

During the first veterinary visit, your pup won't know what to expect. Try to ease his anxiety; you want this first appointment to set a positive tone for all future visits. This will likely be trickier with an adult dog than with a puppy, so be prepared to soothe any nervousness.

The following is a list of several things that must be completed before the day of the appointment:

- Find out how early you need to arrive to complete the paperwork for the new patient.
- Find out if you should bring a stool sample for that first visit. If so, collect it the morning of the visit, and make sure to take it with you.
- Bring the paperwork provided by the breeder or rescue organization for the vet to add to your dog's records.

Your Dalmatian may want to meet the other pups and people in the office and will probably loudly announce your arrival. Although you will

Photo Courtesy of Devin Prudhomme

need to be mindful, this is an opportunity to socialize the puppy and to create a positive experience with the vet. Before letting your puppy meet other animals, always ask the owner for permission and wait for approval. Most pets at the vet's office are likely to not be feeling well, which means they may not be very affable. You don't want a grumpy older dog or a sick animal to nip or scare your puppy. Negative social experiences are situations your puppy will remember; they could make future visits to the vet something to dread. Nor do you want your puppy to be exposed to potential illnesses before he has had all of his shots.

Every vet is different, so you should call your vet ahead of your first visit to get an idea of everything that will be done. Odds are, you will need to bring documentation about your dog, so get your paperwork together when you go to the vet the first time.

Young puppies will need a series of shots. The vet may also request that you bring your dog's latest poop to check it for parasites. Chapter 16 provides more details on what to expect if parasites are detected in your dog's bowel movement.

Be prepared for the vet to ask about your dog's history, even though you just brought the Dalmatian home with you.

During the first visit, the vet will conduct an initial assessment of your Dalmatian. One of the most important things the vet will do is weigh your dog. This is something you are going to have to monitor for your dog's entire life, as you will want to ensure that your Dalmatian remains at a healthy weight. Keep a record of his weight so you can see how quickly your puppy is growing, and to make sure you aren't overfeeding or underfeeding him. Ask your vet what is considered a healthy weight for every growth stage and record that as well.

The vet will set a date for the next group of shots, which will likely happen not too long after the initial visit. After your Dalmatian receives his vaccinations (detailed in Chapter 16), prepare for a couple of days of your puppy feeling under the weather.

- The following are other checks the vet may make during that initial visit.
- Most vets will listen to your dog's heart and lungs to make sure there aren't any obvious problems.
- They will take your pup's temperature, so be prepared to help by calming your dog, as he's probably not going to be happy with this activity.
- Vets usually check a dog's ears, eyes, nose, paws, skin/coat, and genitals.
- They will do a longer check on the mouth and teeth to look for potential problems.
- They will do an initial check on the abdomen and lymph nodes.

If the vet does find a problem and recommends medication, take the time to ask questions and make sure you know what to do before you leave the office.

Crate and Other Preliminary Training

> 66
>
> *We believe in crate training as being the first habit and routine you need to start with your pet. When you are not home, use a kennel for daytime or night sleeping. My dogs willingly go in the crates when they want to feel safe now, and we don't ever have to shut the doors. They should have a safe space just like we do.*
>
> ANNIE SHREVE
> *Dalmatian Creation*
>
> 99

Contrary to what some people think, crates are a safe space for dogs. Crate training will also prepare your dog for occasions when you may have to board him, and he will be put in a crate if you ever travel on a plane.

With a dog like the Dalmatian, there are a few things you can do to make him associate the crate with positivity and security.

Puppies younger than six months should not be left in a crate for hours at a time. Your Dalmatian will not be able to hold his bladder for very long, so you must make sure he has a way to get out and go to the bathroom. If you adopt an adult Dalmatian that is not house-trained, you will need to follow the same rules. If you aren't sure about whether or not the dog is house-trained, it is best to treat the adult as a puppy until you are certain that your newest family member won't use the house as a bathroom.

Make sure the crate door is set so that it doesn't close during your dog's initial sniff of the crate. You do not want your Dalmatian to be scared by the door as it is closing behind him; this could make him fearful of the crate in the future.

The following are some suggestions:

- Use a positive, cheerful voice as you let your Dalmatian sniff the crate for the first time. The first experience in the crate should be associated with excitement and positive emotions. Be sure your dog understands the crate is a good place. If you have a blanket from the puppy's mother, put it in the crate to help provide an extra sense of comfort.

- Drop a couple of treats into the crate if your canine seems reluctant to enter. Do NOT force your dog into the crate. If your dog refuses to go all the way inside the crate, that is perfectly fine. It has to be the dog's decision to enter so that it doesn't become a negative experience.
- Add a toy or two to indicate that the crate is a fun space. These can double for teething toys if you get a puppy—he will need those kinds of toys soon enough, and you want him chewing toys instead of your furniture or nibbling on you.
- For a week or two, feed your dog while he is in the crate. Besides keeping the food away from any other pets, this will create positive associations between your Dalmatian and the crate.
  - If your dog appears comfortable with the crate, put the food all the way at the back.
  - If not, place the food bowl in the front, then move it further back in the crate over time.
- Start closing the door once your dog appears to be eating comfortably in the crate. When the food is gone, open the crate door immediately.
- Leave the door closed for longer periods of time after your dog has finished eating. If your pup begins to whine, you know you have left your Dalmatian in the crate for too long.
- Crate your dog for longer periods of time once the dog shows no signs of discomfort while in the crate when eating. Train your Dalmatian to go into the crate by simply saying, "crate" or "bed." Then praise your dog to let him know that he has done an excellent job.

Repeat these steps for several weeks until your dog seems comfortable in the crate. The regular repetition several times a day teaches your dog that the crate is not a punishment and everything is all right. Initially, you should do this while you are still at home or when you go out to get the mail. When you leave the room, and your puppy lasts half an hour without whining, you can leave the dog alone for longer periods of time. However, keep this alone time to no more than an hour in the beginning.

During the first few weeks, you should also begin to house-train your Dalmatian. Basic behavioral training is also vital from the start. However, wait until your Dalmatian has all of his vaccinations before taking him to structured training classes. Knowledgeable trainers will not accept puppies in their classes until a dog's first full round of shots is complete.

Apart from these initial types of training, you shouldn't be focused on training over the first week. That week should be for bonding. There will be plenty of time for training starting the second week.

Chapters 10 and 11 provide a closer look at how to train your dog.

First-Night Frights

> To prepare a Dalmatian for a new home, I like to advise the new owner to bring a scented blanket from the mother or another familiar pet or owner from the previous home if possible. Dogs need to have a space that is just theirs, with toys and a bed. Make sure your home has a patient and loving atmosphere. Whether we like to believe it or not, the future failure of our pet's behavior is a reflection on ourselves as owners.
>
> REBECCA BIERKO
> *Georgia Dalmatians*

That first night is going to be terrifying for your little Dalmatian puppy! As understandable as this may be, there is only so much comfort you can give your new family member. The more you respond to his cries and whimpering, the more he will learn negative behavior provides the desired results. You need to prepare for a balancing act—one that reassures the Dalmatian that he is safe while keeping him from associating crying with receiving attention from you.

This will be a tough time for your new dog, so here are some recommendations from a couple of breeders.

No two dogs are the same, so you may need to take several different approaches. What is consistent among the recommendations from

Photo Courtesy of
Kaitlynn Martin

breeders is not to give in to those yelps and whines. Once you do, it's over. Your dog is going to know that it will work, and his whining and barking will be endless. Yes, it is going to be incredibly challenging those first few nights, but after a week or two, your dog will learn that nighttime is for sleeping and that you will be there for him—he isn't alone.

Create a sleeping area for your puppy near where you sleep. The area should have the puppy's bed tucked safely into his crate. This will offer him a safe place to hide, where he will feel more comfortable in this strange new home. The entire area should be blocked off to be sure no one can get in (and the puppy can't get out) during the night. This sleeping area should also be close to where people sleep so that the puppy doesn't feel abandoned. If you were able to get a blanket or pillow that smells like the dog's mother, make sure that this is in your puppy's space. Consider adding a little white noise (like an old-fashioned alarm clock) to cover unfamiliar sounds that could scare your new pet.

Your puppy will make noises over the course of the night. Don't move the puppy away, even if the whimpering keeps you awake. Being moved away from people will only scare him more, reinforcing the feeling of anxiety. When your puppy whines during the night, he is not whimpering because he's been in the crate too long. He's scared or wants someone to be with him—he's probably never been alone at night before coming to live with you. Spare yourself trouble later on by teaching the puppy that whimpering will not get him out of the crate. Over time, being close to you at night will be enough to reassure your puppy that everything will be fine.

In the beginning, puppies will need to go to the bathroom every two to three hours. This means you will also need to get up during the night! Make sure your puppy understands he must always go to the bathroom outside or on the pee pad before bedtime. If you ignore this rule, you will have a tough time training your dog to only relieve himself when he is outside and not in the house.

If you choose to let your dog on the bed, wait until he is house-trained. Otherwise, you might have to replace your mattress within a short time. It is best to simply keep your Dalmatian off the furniture so that he doesn't get hurt and your furniture doesn't get ruined!

CHAPTER 8

Introducing Your Dalmatian to Your Other Dogs

Dalmatians can be fantastic family members, but they require socialization and training to keep some of their instincts in check. When properly socialized, they can really love playing with other dogs and animals. They tend to do particularly well on farms, and they love horses. Puppies will be more predictable than adults because you are responsible for their socialization; they are more of a blank slate with other dogs and animals, making it easier to make sure they have positive experiences and learn to enjoy the company of others. An adult will require a much more measured and careful approach unless you know his history with absolute certainty. Some rescues run tests and socialization sessions to see how the dogs will react to other dogs and cats, and they can tell you how well the dog interacts with others. You will still need to approach meeting new dogs with caution, but it can help you to better know what to expect.

Nearly all dogs are hesitant initially when they meet another canine in a completely new environment, regardless if they are puppies or adults. If you have other dogs, it is a chance to begin socializing with your new Dalmatian (Chapter 12).

If you already have a socialized adult dog, your current dog can also help teach your new Dalmatian the rules, and he could even become a mentor to your puppy. If you adopt a puppy, he may imitate your current dog's obedience when you give directions, something that could be really helpful with a potentially stubborn breed. However, this works both ways. If your current dog displays negative behavior, you should try

97

Photo Courtesy of Richard Mathy

to correct these habits before your puppy arrives. You don't want your Dalmatian pup learning bad habits.

As tempting as it may be, it is best not to bring two puppies into the home at the same time, especially from the same litter. They are much more likely to have a stronger bond with each other than with you or your family. Taking on one puppy at a time and having an adult to help you with that puppy is much more likely to have the best results. With a breed like the Dalmatian, two puppies at a time are going to be darn near impossible to handle unless you can be with them full-time for a couple of months. Having one high-energy, intelligent dog is going to be enough of a challenge. Having two means they can play off each other

*Photo Courtesy of
Giovana Pass*

and make things a lot harder, as well as encourage each other to do things you definitely do not want them to do.

Do NOT have your dogs meet at a dog park. A dog park will just be a distraction for the initial meeting because of the number of other dogs coming and going. Find a quieter place to meet, and try to ensure that your dogs can focus on meeting each other instead of trying to go play in the dog area.

FUN FACT
Color Variation

When picturing a Dalmatian, the traditional black and white spotted dog comes to mind. However, Dalmatians can come in several different color variations. These variations can result from recessive genes, including blue, "lemon," brindle, and orange. In addition, a rare tri-color Dalmatian with black and tan spots exists.

Introducing Your New Puppy to Your Other Pets

It doesn't matter what breed your new dog is—introducing him to your current dogs is always something that should be planned and monitored. Even if you feel you know your current dogs, bringing a new dog into the mix can be a challenge. This section details the best way to introduce a puppy to your dogs in an environment that should remove a lot of the potential issues that may make dogs fight.

Introduce all new dogs to your current dog or dogs, regardless of age, in a neutral place away from your home. Even if you have never had problems with your current dog, you are about to change his world. When introducing your dog to the new puppy, select a park or other public area so your current dog will not feel territorial. Neutral ground provides a safer place for all canine parties to start getting to know each other.

When introducing the two dogs, make sure you have at least one other adult with you so that there's one person for each canine. All dogs should be leashed so that you can quickly and easily move them apart if the introduction does not go well. If you have more than two dogs, then you should have one adult per dog. You should not let more than one dog at a time meet your puppy because he may feel overwhelmed. When one of your dogs is through sniffing and meeting the puppy, you can let the next dog have a chance to meet the puppy. Let the dogs take turns meeting the puppy. This will make it easier to keep all of the dogs under control. Even the best dogs can get excited about meeting a puppy. One of the people who needs to be at this meeting is the person who is in charge of the pets in your home. This helps establish the pack hierarchy.

Don't hold your puppy in your arms when the dogs meet. While you may want to protect the puppy, holding him has the opposite effect. Instead, your puppy will feel trapped, but if he is on the ground, he can run if he feels scared. Stand near the puppy with your feet a little bit apart so the dog can hide behind your legs if he decides he needs to escape.

All dogs should have a few minutes to sniff each other, making sure there is always some slack on each leash. Feeling like they can move freely helps dogs to relax, and they won't feel like you are trying to restrain them or force them into something. Your dog may want to play, or he might simply ignore the puppy. You need to let your dog dictate what happens next. If the dogs want to play, be careful your current dog doesn't accidentally hurt the puppy, and if your dog ends up ignoring the puppy after an initial sniff, that is fine too. If your dog is clearly unhappy, keep all of the dogs apart until everyone is comfortable with the meeting. Don't force the situation.

This introduction could take a while, depending on each individual dog's personality. The friendlier and more accepting your current dog is, the easier it will be to incorporate your new puppy into the home. For some dogs, a week is enough time to start feeling comfortable together. For other dogs, it could take a couple of months before they are fully accepting of a new puppy. Since this is a completely new dynamic for your dog, he may be angry with you for bringing this new bundle of energy into his life.

The older your current dog is, the more likely it is that a puppy will be an unwelcome addition. Older dogs can get cranky around a puppy that doesn't know when enough is enough! The goal is to make your puppy feel welcome and safe and to let your older dog know that your love for him is as strong as ever.

Once your new family member and the rest of the canine pack become acquainted and comfortable, you can head home. When you arrive, take the dogs into the yard and remove the leashes. Again, you will need one adult per dog, including the puppy. If the dogs are all right or are indifferent to the puppy, you can let your current dog inside. Then re-leash the puppy, keeping him on the leash as you go inside. This is also a good time to take the puppy to the bathroom before going in so that he knows where to go.

Put the puppy in the puppy area when the introductions are completed. Remember to make sure your current dog cannot get into this area and your puppy cannot get out.

Continuing to expose your puppy or adult dog to your other dogs is going to be important over the next few months. Puppies, in particular, need that socialization to learn not to be overprotective or wary of other pets in your home. Soon that puppy may get to be 70 pounds, bounding around the home, largely unaware of the chaos he causes. Older dogs will almost certainly be annoyed by this. Younger, more energetic dogs may think the puppy is fun, which is great outside, but inside, it is likely to result in damage to your home. All encounters will need to be monitored for a few months until all canines have a more predictable relationship.

Introducing an Adult Dog to Other Pets

If the dog is older, I put it in a crate for 24 hours (only letting it out to go potty). This way other dogs can smell each other safely. I also crate the other dogs and let the 'new' dog roam the house and yard so its scent is all over. Then, after 24 hours, I start introducing the new dog to the pack slowly and one at a time.

HEATHER HENDRICKS
Blazinspots Dalmatians

Photo Courtesy of Terilynn Riley

Always approach the introduction (and the first few weeks together) with caution. The new adult Dalmatian will need his own things from the very beginning—Dalmatians can be territorial if not properly trained. When you aren't around, your dog should be kept in a separate area so there won't be any fighting among the dogs. You may need to be more careful with two adult male dogs as they can be more aggressive and territorial with other males.

Plan for this introduction to take at least an hour. Since the dogs are both adults, they will need to move and become acquainted at their own pace. Since adult Dalmatians are less likely to be friendly initially (if not socialized or accustomed to other dogs), it could take longer. There should be some level of comfort before you leave the park to head home.

When introducing your current dog(s) to your new dog, follow the same steps as you would with a puppy:

- Begin in neutral territory.
- Ask one adult to be present for each adult canine during the introduction.
- Introduce one dog at a time. Don't let several dogs meet your new Dalmatian all at once.

Bring treats to the meeting of two adult dogs—unlike with puppies. The animals will respond to the treats, and if the atmosphere becomes tense, the treats will create a distraction.

During the introduction, watch the Dalmatian and your dog(s) to see if any of them raise their hackles. This is one of the first obvious signs that a dog is uncomfortable. If the Dalmatian's hackles are up, back off the introductions for a little bit. Do this by calling your current dog back first. This is also when you should start waving treats around! Avoid pulling on the leashes to separate the dogs. You don't want to add physical tension to the situation because that could trigger a fight. Treats will work for all dogs, and calling their names should help get things under control.

If any of the dogs are showing their teeth or growling, call your dog back and give the animals a chance to settle down. Use treats and a calming voice to get them to relax. You want all the dogs to feel comfortable during the first meeting, so don't force the friendship. If they seem uncomfortable or wary at first, let them move at their own pace.

Older Dogs and Your Dalmatian

If your current dog is older, keep in mind puppies are energetic, and they want to engage older dogs in play. This can be very trying for your older canine, so make sure your older dog doesn't get too tired of the puppy's antics. A tired older dog could snap and nip at your puppy in hopes of getting a little rest. You don't want your puppy to begin snapping at other dogs too. Watch for signs your older dog is ready for some alone time, some time with you, or simply a break from the puppy. Given how energetic and noisy Dalmatians can be, you want to ensure that your older dog has a place to hide away so that he can relax.

You should always make sure your older dog has safe places to be alone. This is essential for those times when he just doesn't feel up to being around a spry, young puppy! By keeping your puppy and your older dog separated, you can prevent the need for constant scolding. Plus, the puppy will not become wary of older dogs.

Even if you rescue an adult Dalmatian, he might still be too energetic for your older dog to handle. Dalmatians tend to mellow when they mature, but there are some that tend to love being active until they get close to their senior years. Given the size of an adult, that energy will probably come off as incredibly annoying to your older dogs. Be mindful and make sure your dog's golden years are not marred by a new canine that wants to play in a way your older dog can't anymore. Dalmatians are more likely to understand limits faster than a lot of other breeds, but you want to minimize how annoyed your older dog is while your puppy is learning the boundaries.

Dog Aggression and Territorial Behavior

Dalmatians may exhibit a level of dominance or aggression toward dogs they don't know, but usually, this is only a concern when a Dalmatian isn't properly socialized. This is one of the primary reasons why you should never let your Dalmatian off-leash—the other reason being the dog may be a bit too excited and probably won't return because there is too much to explore if he is off-leash. (Details on how to train your Dalmatian are discussed in Chapter 11.)

Dominance aggression is when your dog wants to show control over another animal or person. This kind of aggression can be seen in the following behaviors and in reaction to anyone going near the Dalmatian's belongings (like toys or a food bowl):

Photo Courtesy of Kayla Kaiser

- Growling
- Nipping
- Snapping

This is the behavior that pack leaders use to warn others not to touch their stuff. If you see this reaction in your Dalmatian while he's around you, a family member, or another pet, you must intervene immediately. Correct him by saying, "No," then lavish him with praise when the behavior stops. You must consistently intervene whenever your Dalmatian behaves in this manner.

Do not leave your Dalmatian alone with other people, dogs, or animals as long as any dominance aggression is exhibited. If you are not there to intervene, your dog will push boundaries and will likely try to show his dominance over those around him. Never train your Dalmatians to react aggressively!

Once you are sure this behavior has been eliminated, you can leave your current dog and Dalmatian alone for short periods of time. You should remain in another room or somewhere in close proximity but out of sight. Over time, you can leave your pets alone when you get the mail; then, try leaving them when you run errands or longer tasks. Eventually, you will be able to safely leave your Dalmatian alone with other dogs.

Feeding Time Practices

Your Dalmatian puppy will be fed in his puppy space, so mealtime will not be a problem in the beginning. If you can feed him in his crate, that could be very helpful. However, by the end of the first year, you should be able to have all of your dogs eating in the same area, and that requires some planning and preparation. With a Dalmatian, it will also mean having a towel handy to clean up after all of the slobbering over food.

The following are suggestions for feeding your puppy when the other dogs are present; this will reduce the chances of territorial behavior:

- Feed your Dalmatian at the same time as the other dogs but in a different room. Keeping them separated will let your Dalmatian eat without distractions or feeling that your other dogs will eat what is in his bowl. Make sure to feed your Dalmatian in the same room each time while the other dogs eat in their established areas.
- Keep your Dalmatian and other dogs in their areas until they finish eating their food. Some dogs have a tendency to leave food in the bowl. Don't let them. They need to finish everything because all food bowls will be removed as soon as the dogs finish eating. If food is left, get the bowl off the ground.
- Make sure you have someone near your Dalmatian so that the dog learns not to growl at people near the bowl. This will help reduce stress when other dogs are around the food. If your dog demonstrates any aggression, immediately correct him by saying, "No," and then give praise when the behavior stops. Do not play with the food bowl, and make sure none of the kids play with it. Your dog needs to know that no one is going to try to steal his food.
- Over the course of a couple of weeks, move your dogs closer together while they are eating. For example, you can feed your current dog on one side of the door near the doorway and the Dalmatian on the opposite side.

After a month or two, you can feed the dogs in the same room but with some distance between them. If your Dalmatian starts to exhibit protective behavior with the other dogs, correct the Dalmatian, and then praise him when he stops the behavior.

Eventually, you can start feeding the dogs close to one another. This can take weeks to months to accomplish, depending on the age of the Dalmatian and his personality. A puppy will need less time because he will be socialized with the dogs from an early age, making him less wary that the other dogs will try to take his food. That does not mean he won't display territorial behavior. Yet, it likely won't take long for him to start to feel comfortable eating near the rest of the pack.

For adult dogs, this process could take longer—don't rush it! Let your dog learn to feel comfortable eating before you make changes, even small ones. Dogs of any breed can be protective of their food, depending on their past history. Before your dog will eat peacefully, he must be assured that his protective behavior is not necessary around other dogs. That means letting his confidence and comfort level build at his own pace.

Cleaning up behind your Dalmatian's meal can be helpful. Any slobber and water on the floor could be a slippery hazard, and slobber on the walls will build up and create discoloration over time. This is a consideration for many dogs because some breeds slobber a lot more than others, but with a dog as big as a Dalmatian, the mess is going to be a lot more obvious after every meal. The cleanup won't take long—just a quick wipe down, then you can get back to having fun with your dog.

CHAPTER 9

The First Few Weeks

Since they are incredibly active dogs, time is going to fly by with your Dalmatian. Every day can be an adventure, and you will be able to do all kinds of enjoyable activities with your dog, which means that before you know it, years will have passed. That starts with the day you bring home your Dalmatian and see that initial caution and curiosity as he starts to explore your home.

No matter what age your dog is, his unique personality will start to show, and you'll learn what kinds of rewards and incentives work well in getting your Dalmatian to listen to you. It is important to remember not to get too reliant on treats during these early days, something that is going to be difficult. Dalmatians are incredibly food-driven dogs, and it will be tempting to use that when your Dalmatian starts to show any signs of being headstrong or willful. There are other ways of convincing your dog to listen, and that will start in the first few weeks after your dog arrives.

It is best to expect the process to be a lot of work because it often is when you bring home a new dog. That first week will be a challenge as you try to train your dog while making sure he feels comfortable in his new surroundings. Leaving his previous home, even for a rescue, is going to make the dog apprehensive about being somewhere new. There are a lot of things to do (and some things to avoid) to help your dog ease into the new environment and really bring out his excited, active, and loving personality. During that first week, it is all about helping your dog feel comfortable enough not to be wary of the new setting.

As mentioned in the previous chapter, there shouldn't be much training outside of crate training and house-training during those first few weeks. Puppies don't listen during the early days when the instructions aren't for something they do naturally. They will definitely need to use the bathroom and eat, so crate training and house-training are things they will understand. Also, they haven't learned to listen to you yet. You can avoid creating a negative training environment by giving yourself and your dog time to get acquainted before you dive into other types of training. Don't worry; your dog isn't really going to lose time because Dalmatians are clever. With your bond established, it will be easier to get your dog to take you seriously instead of being wary around you.

Photo Courtesy of Autumn Werner

With their intelligence, Dalmatians will likely quickly understand their new surroundings as they learn that this is their new home. When your dog is not sleeping, you may find yourself feeling that you can't get a moment's rest—but in a fun and entertaining way. The bond you and your Dalmatian form in those early days will be important in establishing the relationship you have over the years.

By the end of the first month, your pup should be sleeping through the night, which will be an absolute blessing considering how difficult those first few days tend to be. House-training can be very easy when it is done right, but without the right approach, it can be a real chore. Having a great breeder who starts the process will further speed up how quickly your little one learns. You will want to monitor your Dalmatian, though, and never let a puppy or dog out of the dedicated area alone during the first week and probably, a good bit longer.

The first month is when you really need to start paying attention to your puppy's emerging personality. As with all intelligent breeds, the key is to remain consistent when it comes to training. That means everyone should be consistent, including the kids. Always use what you learn about your puppy's personality to encourage good behavior!

Setting the Rules and Sticking to Them – NO Exceptions

> "
>
> *Dalmatians thrive on repetition. This means that your Dalmatian should start becoming familiar with your routine as soon as possible. Learning when breakfast and dinner are, and when playtime, walk time, and other day-to-day activities are, is extremely important.*
>
> FANNY FIDDLER
> *North Paw Dalmatians*
>
> "

If a Dalmatian sees that people are willing to compromise, they are going to exploit that as much as possible. If you give in during that first week, you are giving the dog an unintentional lesson—how to get you to do what *he* wants. A good rule for any breed, but especially for more intelligent dogs, is to always set the rules and a schedule and don't allow any deviation. This goes for both your dog and your kids, regardless of the age of the dog or child. You don't want your older children or teens undoing your hard work by letting the new Dalmatian out of the puppy's dedicated area to roam around unattended. Make sure everyone knows that the rules apply to everyone.

Rules are not the same as more traditional training. The rules are the same as the kinds of rules you give your children; other types of training are more like what kids learn in school. It's never too early to start teaching your dog the rules.

Your puppy needs to understand the rules and know you and your family mean them, even if the dog really doesn't like what you are saying. Once your canine learns to follow your commands, there will still be times when he will refuse to obey. That is nearly a certainty. However, he will be much more likely to listen once he knows you are in control.

Do *not* allow yourself or anyone in your family to think that making an exception is all right, no matter how cute those eyes are. Once a

Dalmatian realizes that certain rules are negotiable, it will be incredibly difficult to teach him otherwise. The best reward is positive reinforcement, not breaking the rules.

Establish a No Jumping and No Mouthing Policy

No matter how cute your puppy might be, you definitely want to start training your dog not to jump up on people because once he reaches his full height and weight, he will be able to knock people off their feet. If not properly trained, a Dalmatian may jump up on you in greeting, and this can be very bad if the dog tries to jump up on little children or frail adults. Such a muscular build means the dog can easily knock over a toddler unintentionally. You have the responsibility of ensuring that your dog and children learn how to play properly. For your Dalmatian, this means no jumping up on people.

Nor do you want a puppy to feel it is all right to mouth you because when your dog is fully grown, his mouth is going to be big. Any games that involve biting or nipping should always be avoided. You do not want your Dalmatian to ever think that nipping is all right. This will be very difficult if you don't enforce the rule right from the beginning.

Photo Courtesy of Katie Peltier

Nipping

Although they aren't generally aggressive, Dalmatians (or any dog) are likely to nip under two conditions.

- One of the triggers for nipping is overstimulation. This can be one sign your puppy is too tired to keep playing or training, and you should put him to bed.

- Another trigger could be that your canine has too much energy. If this is the case, take your puppy outside to burn off some of his excess energy. At the same time, be careful not to over-exercise the puppy.

You need to be vigilant and immediately let your puppy know nipping is not acceptable. Some people recommend using a water spritzer bottle and spraying the puppy while saying "No," after nipping. This is one of the few times when punishment may be effective, and it is probably essential. Remember—make sure your dog does not associate the spraying with anything other than his nipping. He needs to understand that he is getting sprayed because he is nipping someone and that this is not acceptable behavior.

Always firmly tell your puppy, "No," whenever he is nipping, even if it is during playtime. You should also pull away and loudly say, "Ouch!" to let your puppy know his teeth are hurting you. This will help to establish the idea that nipping is bad and is never rewarded.

Chewing

> *A new puppy needs a routine. Dalmatians can be stubborn; give them time, and most of all, put your shoes and valuables away. Teething can be troublesome for new owners, and some choose to get rid of their puppy after it rips the couch or tears up favorite clothing. This phase will go away, and frozen applesauce bites or leather chews work wonders. Once they get into a routine of exercise, it will get easier. If a puppy is getting into trouble, more often than not it's not being taken care of the way it needs to be taken care of.*
>
> REBECCA BIERKO
> *Georgia Dalmatians*

All puppies chew to relieve the pain of teething. Whether your dog is chewing on your furniture or clothing, be sure to discourage this behavior as quickly as possible:

- Make sure you have toys for your Dalmatian (whether an adult or a puppy) so that you can teach him which objects are acceptable for chewing. Having a lot of available toys and rotating those toys out will give your puppy or dog several options.
- If your puppy is teething, either refrigerate a couple of toys so that they are cold or give your puppy frozen carrots. The cold will help to numb the pain. Teething usually starts between three and four months old, and it usually ends by eight months. You want to get toys that will be safe for your dog's teeth.
- Toys that are made of hard rubber or hard nylon are best, particularly Kongs with kibble in them. You can even fill them with water and freeze them, which will give your puppy something cool to soothe the pain of teething.

For the most part, keeping an eye on your dog when he is not in his designated space will help you quickly see when he is chewing on things he shouldn't. When this happens, firmly say, "No." If your dog continues to chew, put him back in his space. While he is in the space, make sure he has plenty of toys to chew on.

If you decide to use chew deterrents, such as bitter training sprays, be aware some dogs will not care if an item tastes bad—they will chew on it anyway. If you apply these deterrents, do not leave your dog alone and expect him to stop chewing. You should watch your dog's reaction before trusting that the bad habit is broken. Since some Dalmatians have separation anxiety, you should eliminate the chewing problem as quickly as possible; this will allow your pup to roam freely around your home.

Jumping

You should not allow your Dalmatian to jump up on other people or animals. A cute little puppy will be able to knock down full-grown adults within a year, and this can be detrimental to everyone involved. Use the

Photo Courtesy of
Hailey Kesler

following steps when you have a visitor. If you can, get someone who is willing to help you because that will make training that much easier; two people will be able to better handle a large dog.

1. Put a leash on the dog when the person knocks on the door or rings the bell. The arrival of someone will invariably excite most dogs, especially puppies.
2. Let the person in, but do not approach the visitor until your pup calms down.
3. Be effusive in your praise when the puppy keeps all four paws on the ground.
4. If the puppy jumps up on the visitor, the visitor should turn his body and ignore the dog. Don't verbally correct the dog. Being completely ignored will be far more of a deterrent than any words you can say.
5. Give your dog something to hold in his mouth if he does not settle down. Sometimes dogs just need a task to reduce their excitement. A stuffed animal or a ball is an ideal distraction, even if your dog drops it.
6. At this point, the visitor can get down to the dog's level and pet your dog. Having someone on his level will make your Dalmatian feel he is being included. It also lets him sniff the visitor's face, which is part of a proper greeting to a dog. If your visitor is willing to help, this acknowledgment can prevent your pup from further jumping since he already feels safe with the person who is at his level.

Reward-Based Training Versus Discipline-Based Training

With an intelligent breed like the Dalmatian, it is much more efficient to train your puppy using rewards than with punishments. This will be a particular challenge as puppies can be exuberant and easily distracted. It is important to remember that your puppy is young, so you need to keep your temper and learn when a break from training is needed. Since Dalmatians are interested in pleasing their people, positive attention can be incredibly effective in getting your dog to listen to you.

The following are several critical training aspects you will need to address during the first month:

- House-training (Chapter 10)
- Crate training (Chapter 6)
- Barking (Chapter 11)

Find out how much house-training was completed by the breeder. The best breeders may teach puppies one or two commands before the puppy goes home with you. If this is the case, keep using those same commands with your puppy so that the early training is not lost. This information can help you establish the right tone of voice to use with your puppy since he will already know what the words mean and how to react to them.

How Long Is Too Long to Be Left Home Alone?

Dalmatians suffer from separation anxiety, and that means leaving them home alone for long periods of time is not advised. Some of them can learn to be all right while you are away for a full workday. Others never seem to get to the point where hours of separation are easy to take.

In the beginning, your dog should spend only a brief period of time in the crate while you are gone. Dalmatians have been companions since they were first bred, so they do not like to be left home alone. This is why it is best to make sure they have a companion. As your dog becomes house-trained and trustworthy, you should allow him to leave the crate while you are gone so that he doesn't feel he is being punished. Your new companion will not do well trapped in a crate for hours at a time. That said, in an emergency, a dog can be all right in a crate for up to eight hours without a person as long as you have made sure to allow the dog to burn off energy first.

You also need to find some good mental games that will keep your pup occupied while you are gone. Brain games can keep your dog hap-pily occupied while you are away, and having another dog can provide stimulation (though you may want to make sure to tire them both out before leaving, and the companion dog must also be well-socialized and not of the same gender).

As an adult, your Dalmatian will probably be highly active. As a puppy, your Dalmatian will go from sleeping to being rambunctious to sleeping again, all within a brief period of time. A tired puppy is a lot like a tired toddler; you have to keep the little guy from becoming exhausted or from overworking those short little legs (while

HELPFUL TIP
Dalmatian Crying

Dalmatians are renowned for their range of vocalizations. This range of sounds goes beyond barking and includes the infamous Dalmatian cry. This distinctive sound is a high-pitched whine and can be pretty startling if you're unfamiliar with these dogs. The Dalmatian cry can indicate anxiety, excitement, fear, or boredom. Canine body language is an important tool for interpreting this variable cry. Understanding and analyzing this vocalization can help you bond with your Dalmatian.

they are still short). You need to be careful about harming your puppy's growing bones. Your pup is probably going to think that sleep is unnecessary, no matter how tired he is. It is up to you to read the signs that tell you when to stop all activities and take a break or put your pup to bed.

You should train your dog in increments of time—only for the amount of time that he can handle. Don't push your puppy's training past his concentration level, and don't discourage your adult dog by using commands that are too advanced. If you continue training your puppy past his energy levels, the lessons learned are not going to be the ones you want to teach your dog. At this age, training sessions don't need to be long; they just need to be consistent.

Walks will be much shorter during the first month. When you go outside, stay within a few blocks of home. Don't worry—by the month's end, your puppy will have more stamina, and you will be able to enjoy longer walks with your new friend. You can also do a bit of walking on the leash in the yard if your puppy has lots of extra energy. Puppies have a tendency to attack their leash while walking because it is a distraction from running freely. Taking walks will also help your Dalmatian learn how to behave on the leash.

Photo Courtesy of
Brianna Quigley

Just because your puppy can't endure long walks initially doesn't mean he won't have plenty of energy. Daily exercise will be essential, with the caveats that you need to make sure your puppy isn't doing too much too soon and that he doesn't get too hot (they do handle warmer climates well) or too cold in colder climates. Staying active will not only keep him healthy, but it will also keep him mentally stimulated. You will quickly realize how sedentary your "non-puppy life" has been because you will be on the move the entire time your puppy is awake!

PART 3

Training and Activities

CHAPTER 10

House-Training

> **"**
>
> *Prepare to not ever leave your puppy alone for too long. A good way to keep an eye on your puppy and to also teach it the boundaries in the home is to have it tethered to you. This is also great for potty training and you'll have a lot fewer accidents. This little pup is going to have you running all over your home unless you have a way to help it settle. Tethering is your best option whenever you have the puppy out and about.*
>
> TERI L. PETRE
> *Dalmatian Palace of the Northwest*
>
> **"**

One of the first questions that people ask when adopting a Dalmatian puppy (or any other breed) is how easy they are to house-train. It's a fair question, and the answer for Dalmatians is that it really depends on the dog. As a general rule, they are considered one of the easier breeds to train, but that doesn't mean that your individual dog will fit into a typical experience. This is a dog that is known for being stubborn and playful, bordering on mischievous.

As you approach this less-than-pleasant aspect of training your Dalmatian, it's best to have the mindset that there will be times when it is easy, but you will face some challenges as you go. Even if it is nobody's favorite task, everyone can appreciate the successful end results of house-training a puppy. After those first few months, the effort will be more than worth it when you no longer have to worry about hidden messes around your home.

FUN FACT
Largest Litter

The world record for the largest litter of Dalmatian puppies is 19 puppies. This litter was born in Albury, Australia, on June 13, 2019, via C-Section. All puppies survived and were given names inspired by Disney films.

You need to treat house-training with the same kind of patience and consistency that you apply to other types of training. This does tend to be more difficult because we want to punish "bad behavior," but in the early days, a dog using the inside of the house to do his business isn't "bad"—it's natural. Consider that humans aren't even able to be potty trained until they can walk, which is usually about two years after they are born—six months doesn't seem quite so long when you put it in perspective. Keep in mind that your Dalmatian isn't misbehaving or intentionally disobeying you; he is learning where to go to the restroom, which is a lot harder than learning how to sit. To speed up the process, be patient, and praise your dog when he goes in the right place. Your dog wants to please you, so treats and positive reinforcement will go a long way to getting your Dalmatian to use the outside for all his potty business.

The recommended age to start house-training a Dalmatian is between eight and 12 weeks. It's likely the breeder will have started the process before you bring home your puppy, so you may want to use the same method that they used. If your dog comes home earlier than that, you probably aren't going to see much progress in those early days, but you can start showing him other dogs going outside to relieve themselves.

While you are trying to train the dog on where to use the bathroom, you will almost certainly see him trying to decide if he *should* listen to you. All it takes is one time when you allow yourself to be distracted, and you can turn house-training into an incredibly difficult chore. But if you can keep your focus while remaining consistent and firm, your Dalmatian should be trained by the time he's six months old.

Staying focused when you have your dog outside for a restroom break isn't necessarily enough; if you fail to keep a constant eye on your puppy when he is exploring inside your home, be prepared for a lot of messes. Puppies will sneak off to use the bathroom inside if you let your attention stray.

*Photo Courtesy of
Amy Lawson*

This is when learning to be firm and consistent is really going to count, and sticking to the rules will be absolutely essential. You will also need to remain calm and patient; getting upset will only reinforce undesirable behavior. The best tool in house-training a potentially stubborn breed is to set a schedule and stick to it—no deviations! Once your dog realizes you are staying focused and that you will get him outside for a break, he will accept that rule and do what he's supposed to do.

Leashing your Dalmatian to go outside can help show your puppy where and when to go to the bathroom—even in your yard. However, there will still be challenges.

The following is a list of rules to apply when house-training your puppy:

- Never let the puppy roam the house alone—he should always be in his dedicated puppy space when you are not watching him. No Dalmatian wants to spend a lot of time in a soiled crate, so being in his crate is a deterrent from doing his business there when you are not around. He may not feel the same way about other areas of your home if he is free to wander.

- Give your puppy constant, easy access to his designated bathroom spaces. You will need to make frequent trips outside with your puppy as he learns where to do his business.
- When you go outside, put a leash on your puppy to make a point of where in the yard you want him to use the bathroom.
- If your puppy doesn't potty within a few minutes, take him inside and put him in the crate for a few minutes. Then take him back outside to make sure he does go to the bathroom. This isn't punishment for the puppy but a break in case he was getting too distracted to focus on going to the bathroom. Once all stimuli are removed, and he's in his crate, he may realize that he does have some business to take care of.

Always begin with a training plan; then, be even stricter with yourself than you are with your puppy when keeping to the schedule. You are the key to your puppy's learning!

Inside or Outside – House-Training Options and Considerations

> 66
>
> *Having a schedule of trips outside to support house-training is essential. Like any puppies, Dalmatian pups need to go out after eating, when they wake up, and any time it has been a while since they were outside. You should never restrict water with any breed of puppy, as they can become dehydrated very easily. Consistent access to water is even more essential for Dalmatians. The best way to combat this is healthy hydration and frequent trips outside. Be prepared to get up in the middle of the night for a potty break. Start good habits early!*
>
> HEATHER PARSONS
> *Bedlam Acres Dalmatians*
>
> 99

If your breeder has already started the house-training process, make sure to coordinate your training so that you pick up where the breeder left off. Having someone who really knows how to house-train a dog can give you a huge leg up on the whole endeavor—take it if you can get it!

Photo Courtesy of Heiarii Robson Snyder

The following is a list of house-training options for your puppy:

- Pee pads – You should have several around the home for training, including in the puppy's area but as far from his bed as possible.
- Regular outings – Organize these outings based on your puppy's sleeping and eating schedule.
- Rewards – You can use treats in the beginning but quickly shift to praise.

Setting a Schedule

You need to keep an eye on your puppy and always follow his meals, before and after sleep, and before and after being in his crate, with house-training sessions. Watch for cues like sniffing and circling, which are two common signs a puppy exhibits when searching for a place to go potty. Start tailoring your schedule around your puppy's unique needs. Puppies have small bladders and little control in the early days—so at this time, it isn't stubbornness but ability that is making it difficult for your puppy to follow your directions.

If you train your Dalmatian to do his business inside, you need a designated space in the puppy's area for a clean pee pad. Pee pads are better than newspapers and can absorb more. Make sure you change the pads regularly so that your puppy does not get accustomed to having waste nearby. Even if you use pee pads, you should plan to transition your dog to doing his business outdoors as quickly as possible.

Choosing a Location

> "
> *Toilet training is the most important thing the first couple weeks, and if a new owner is consistent and committed to this, toilet training will probably only take a few days. Some Dals need a bit more time, but not much if you get them outside after eating, take them to the same location, and use the same words to tell them what you want them to do. And when they do, praise them generously. Interact with them and talk to them a lot. Playing music is also very good for Dalmatians as it stimulates their senses and soothes them.*
>
> LAURA FOWLER
> *Classic Dalmatians*
> "

A designated bathroom space will make the house-training experience easier because your Dalmatian will associate one area of the yard with that specific purpose. Having him use one spot every time will also make clean-up simpler, and you will be able to use the entire yard instead of having to worry about stepping in dog waste.

The perfect time to train your puppy to go to the bathroom is when you go out for walks. Between walks and using the yard, your puppy will come to see the leash as a sign that it is time to relieve his bladder, which could become a Pavlovian response.

Do not send your puppy outside alone and assume he has done what you want him to do. He needs to understand the purpose of going outside is to go to the bathroom. Until there are no more accidents in the house, you need to be sure your puppy is not losing focus. With a breed like the Dalmatian, it is best to always verify that your little fellow follows through. If it is too hot or cold outside, and you don't make sure he takes care of business, you run the risk that he will take advantage of that lack of supervision to pretend he has done his business just so he can get back inside faster. Then accidents are nearly guaranteed, even if you thought that your dog was fully house-trained.

Keyword Training

> *Be consistent! I teach all my dogs a command for potty. My command is 'hurry, hurry.' Every time I take the pup out to the bathroom, which is quite often, I tell it, Hurry, hurry. I stay there until it goes. Once it goes, I praise it with a treat and tell it, 'Good hurry, hurry!' and take it back inside. Some pups learn very quickly; others not so fast, but they all eventually get it.*
>
> BARBARA ALLISON
> *Rim Rock Dalmatians*

You and all family members should consistently use key words when house-training your dog. If you have paired an adult with a child, the adult should be the one using the key word during training.

To avoid confusing your puppy, be careful not to select words that you often use inside the home. Use a phrase like "Get busy" to let your puppy know it's time to do his business. Do not use words like "bathroom" or "potty" because these words are sometimes used in casual conversation, which could trigger a desire in your dog to go to the bathroom. "Get busy" is not a phrase most people use in their daily routine, so it is not something you are likely to say unless you want your puppy to go to the bathroom outside.

Once your puppy learns to use the bathroom based on the command, make sure he finishes before offering praise or rewards.

*Photo Courtesy of
Reece Hunter*

Reward Good Behavior with Positive Reinforcement

Dalmatians are incredibly receptive to positive reinforcement, making it highly effective for all kinds of training (not just house-training). In the beginning, take a few pieces of kibble with you when you are teaching your puppy where to go, both inside and outside the home. Learning you are the one in charge will help teach your Dalmatian to look to you for cues and instructions.

Part of being consistent with training means lavishing the little guy with praise whenever your puppy does the right thing. Use a leash to gently lead your puppy to his bathroom area, with no stops in between.

It will gradually become obvious to your Dalmatian that this is where he should go to use the bathroom. Once you get outside, encourage your pup to go only when you get to the place in the yard that is intended for his bathroom spot. As soon as he does his business, give him immediate and very enthusiastic praise. Pet your puppy as you talk, and let the little guy know just how good the action was. Once the praise is done, return inside immediately. This is not playtime. You want your puppy to associate certain outings with designated potty time.

You can also give your puppy a treat after a few successful trips outside. Definitely do not make treats a habit after each trip because you do not want your Dalmatian to expect one every time he does his business. The lesson is to go outside, not to receive a treat every time.

The best way to house-train in the first couple of months is to go out every hour or two, even during the night. Set an alarm to wake yourself during the night so that you remember to take the puppy outside. Use the leash to keep the focus on using the bathroom, give the same enthusiastic praise, then immediately return inside and go back to bed. It is difficult, but your Dalmatian will get the hang of it a lot faster if there isn't a lengthy period between potty breaks. Over time, the pup will need to go outside less frequently.

Cleaning Up

Once a dog goes to the bathroom in your home, that odor will remain there for other dogs to smell, even if it's not detectable to your own nose after you've cleaned the area thoroughly. Your Dalmatian might take any lingering odor as a sign that the spot is an acceptable place to use the bathroom.

This means you have to be very diligent about handling accidents:
- Clean up any messes in the house as soon as you find them.
- In areas where your dog has an accident, thoroughly clean the spot so that there is no remaining scent.

Spend a bit of time researching what kind of cleaner you want to use, whether generic or holistic. For example, you will probably want to get

Photo Courtesy of Theresa Ledford

a product with an enzyme cleaner. Enzymes help to remove stains by speeding up the chemical reaction of the cleaner with the stain. They also help to remove the smell faster, which reduces the odds your dog will continue to go to the bathroom in the same place. If your Dalmatian is properly trained, he will feel no need to mark his territory, but you should also discourage other dogs from claiming areas around your property.

If your Dalmatian has an accident, it is important to refrain from punishing the puppy. Punishment simply teaches your dog to hide his mess or to be stealthier about when he does his business inside. Accidents are not a reason to punish. If they happen often, it is really more of a reflection of your training and your schedule than the puppy. However, even the best trainers can tell you accidents are pretty much an inevitability. When it happens, tell your puppy, "No! Potty outside!" and clean up the mess immediately. Once you have finished cleaning up the mess, take the puppy outside. It

Photo Courtesy of
Rebekah Luno

isn't likely that he will need to go potty again, but it is worth the attempt in case he still has a little left.

Pay attention to when these accidents happen and determine if there is a commonality between them. Perhaps you need to add an extra trip outside during the day for your puppy, or you should make a change in his walking schedule. Or maybe there is something that is startling your dog and causing an accident.

Remember, this is a dog that is loyal and loves his people. As a people-pleaser, it is far easier to get a Dalmatian house-trained faster. If you get upset, that will upset your dog, resulting in more accidents. If you can stay calm and patient, house-training isn't going to be the nightmare that it can be with a lot of other breeds.

CHAPTER 11

Training Your Dalmatian

> " Dalmatians are independent thinkers. They are not people pleasers by nature. You have to give them a positive incentive and help them figure out how to get it. I recommend clicker training or other free-choice positive-reinforcement training. This can be very easy: Hold up the food dish until puppy sits, then give the food. Don't waste your breath saying, Sit ... sit ... sit ... Just wait and the dog will eventually figure it out. Multiple short training sessions (five minutes, five times a day) are much better than one long one.
>
> SARAH GROTE, DVM
> *Willing Hearts Dalmatian Rescue* "

It is impossible to predict how easy or difficult it will be to train your Dalmatian for other tasks. That high desire to make you happy will be pitted against a willful stubbornness that rivals that of a toddler. Fortunately, your approach will play a large role in how easy the training will be. As long as you are consistent, kind, give as much praise as treats, and are regular with your training, training will not be nearly so much of a chore.

Since Dalmatians are intelligent, they don't tend to take that long to put two and two together. While you will need to be mindful of how many treats you give your Dalmatian when he's a puppy, he's going to be growing really fast, so getting the basics down quickly may mean giving him a lot of treats. Over time, you can move to praise (it will be pretty effective, too) as the primary reward, but when dealing with a dog as big as a Dalmatian, giving puppies more treats is all right. If you have an adult Dalmatian that needs training, though, you are going to have to go light on the treats and primarily offer praise.

Positive attention and extra play are fantastic rewards for a loving dog like the Dalmatian, so training is still going to be relatively easy. As they are dogs that are very sensitive to any negativity, it is best not to agitate them because that will make them less likely to understand or do what you want.

It is absolutely essential to ensure that your Dalmatian learns the basic commands covered in these chapters for his protection and for that of your visitors. Given his size, a Dalmatian can get carried away and knock people over without any understanding of how dangerous his actions are.

Early Training is a Must

> "
>
> *Dalmatians can be very food motivated, which can make training easy. However, the breed can also be known to be slightly stubborn. It is important that the owner establishes who is in charge, as well as sets boundaries with the Dalmatian.*
>
> FANNY FIDDLER
> *North Paw Dalmatians*
> "

All large dogs require early training because of the risks they pose if they don't learn how to behave. From knocking people over to literally running over children, large dogs are more likely to accidentally harm others. It can be difficult to stay composed when a dog keeps jumping up on people because most people don't know how to deal with this kind of behavior in an effective way. The natural reaction is to give a dog attention, even if it is to try to convince him to stay down. Training him early, before he spends much time outside with others, will help you to get some of the bad behaviors worked out. Given how different Dalmatians look from most other breeds, you'll find that a lot of people will approach your dog out of curiosity. Your Dalmatian will probably be just as curious about them, so you want to make sure that you are able to keep all four of his paws on the ground during social interactions.

Best Practices and Benefits to Keep in Mind before You Start

> **"**
>
> *Dalmatians are smart but get bored easily. They want to please you, but don't respond well to harsh training methods. Training has to be fun for them. They expect a partner, not a drill sergeant. Once they understand what you want, they will do it until it isn't fun anymore. Keep them guessing and you both will be happy.*
>
> BARBARA ALLISON
> *Rim Rock Dalmatians*
>
> **"**

In the early days, be prepared to keep your frustration levels in check. Your dog has to be convinced that you are in charge and that you mean business—and he needs to know the reward for that is a lot of fun. If you take out your frustration on your Dalmatian, you are teaching him that training isn't fun. Whether you bring a puppy or an adult dog into your home, he has to learn the boundaries in a way that is safe and shows patience, just like teaching a child. If you take a few minutes to watch training videos of Dalmatians before you bring one home and as you prepare to start training, that will give you a good idea of what you could be in for when you start to train your newest family member.

Just remember—being firm, consistent, and patient will go a long way. Don't let that adorable face sway you from getting your pup to do what you instruct him to do. He will be just as happy a little way down the road if you stick to it now. And that happy face when playing with you is priceless.

HELPFUL TIP
Natural Athletes

Dalmatians possess innate athleticism, making them naturally adept at physical activities. In addition, their muscular build, natural agility, and endurance make them excellent competitors in canine sports and training endeavors. Due to their high energy, Dalmatians thrive with regular exercise opportunities. By engaging these high-energy dogs in activities that utilize their intelligence, such as agility training, obedience training, or dog sports, you'll help fulfill their need for physical and mental stimulation. In addition, incorporating a healthy diet of physically and mentally stimulating activities will ensure a happy, well-rounded pup.

Always make the early training sessions short, no matter how old your dog is. Those training sessions are as much about learning how your Dalmatian will respond to training as they are about actually training your dog. Puppies won't have the ability to keep focused like adults, so a short session is ideal for keeping them from learning to ignore you. Adult dogs are going to be suspicious of you (though you may also get an adult that is already familiar with training, which could make training a little easier). And odds are, you are going to be quite tired by the end of those sessions—you'll be just as relieved as your pup is to be done. As long as you are firm and consistent during those early sessions, keeping them short is in everyone's best interest.

Training will be slow going in the beginning, as your dog will be quite excited about the interaction. Don't take this as an indication of your puppy's interest levels—it's more indicative of his inexperience. If you are patient with your pup from the start, you will find it will pay off later.

Training is as important as socialization, and it can make general excursions easier; more importantly, training could be a way of saving your dog's life. Understanding commands might prevent your dog from running into the street, responding to provocations from other dogs, or acting territorial.

Training can also really benefit your relationship with your pup because it is a wonderful way to bond. This dedicated time together helps you understand your puppy's developing personality as you learn what kind of reward will work best for other tasks. Be sure your Dalmatian is well-trained so you can enjoy a full range of activities together—from picnics to outings in the park!

Choosing the Right Reward

> *Dalmatians are very clever, biddable, and eager to learn. Like many smart breeds, they can get bored repeating the same command over and over. They do best working for short periods of time on one behavior before moving on to something new. Most Dalmatians love food and treats and will work happily for these rewards.*
>
> HEATHER PARSONS
> *Bedlam Acres Dalmatians*

Treats are the easiest way of keying a puppy into the idea that performing tricks is good behavior, but ultimately you want your little one to follow commands without expecting food. Soon, you will need to switch to a reward that is a secondary reinforcer. Praise, additional playtime, and extra petting are all fantastic rewards for your Dalmatian. Your dog will probably follow you around until you decide to just sit back and relax. Plopping down to watch a movie and letting your puppy sit with you is a great reward after an intense training session.

Make sure you switch from treats to a different kind of positive reward as early as possible. Since many Dalmatians love their toys, you don't have to rely solely on treats as a method of praise.

If you would like your Dalmatian to connect positive feedback with a sound, you can use a clicker. This training tool is relatively inexpensive and should be used at the same time as you praise your puppy or dog. Clickers are not necessary, but some trainers find them useful.

Photo Courtesy of Cody Ifland

Name Recognition

Using a dog's name is going to be the first part of training your dog. Over time, many of us create different names for our dogs. Nicknames can be used later. However, before you can train a dog, you have to make sure he understands his real name. In the beginning, you will use your dog's name to get his attention, and that will be the indicator for the Dalmatian to look at you for what to do next.

The following list provides some name-recognition suggestions:

1. Get some treats and show one to your dog.
2. Say the dog's name and immediately say, "Yes." (Your dog should be looking at you when you speak.) Then give your dog a treat.
3. Wait 10 seconds, then show your dog a treat and repeat step two.

Sessions shouldn't last longer than about five minutes because your dog will lose focus or interest. Name recognition is something you can do several times each day. After you have done this for five to 10 sessions, the training will change a bit:

1. Wait until your dog isn't paying attention to you.
2. Call your dog. If he has a leash on, give it a gentle tug to get your dog's attention.
3. Say, "Yes," and give the dog a treat when he looks at you.

During this time, do not speak your dog's name when you correct him or for any reason other than name recognition. This is because, in the beginning, you need to get the dog to associate his name only with something positive, like treats. This will more quickly program your dog to listen to you no matter what else is going on around him.

It is likely that your Dalmatian will not require a lot of time before he recognizes his name. Repetition while looking at your pup is a great way to speed up the learning process.

Essential Commands

There are seven basic commands that all dogs should know (Sit, Down, Stay, Come, Leave It, Drop It, and Heel). These commands are the basis for a happy and enjoyable relationship with your dog, as well as giving you a way to keep your dog safe and out of trouble. Then, there are some commands that are incredibly helpful, like "Off" if you don't want pets on the furniture and "Quiet" for a noisy dog.

Train your puppy to do the commands in the order they appear in this chapter. The last two commands are optional since you may allow your dog to be on the furniture, and you may not mind a vocal canine. Since dogs sit often, "Sit" is the easiest command to teach, making it the best starting point. Teaching "Leave It" and "Drop It" is much more difficult and usually requires the puppy to fight an instinct or a desire. Consider how often you give in to something you want, even when you know you shouldn't! That's pretty much what your puppy is facing.

"Quiet" can be another difficult command, as dogs (particularly puppies) tend to bark in response to their surroundings. Some puppies do grow out of the constantly barking stage. If you finish all the other commands and find that your dog is still a bit too noisy for your home, you can then start training him to be quiet, though you will need to determine just when you want him to be quiet and when you want him to bark (like when someone is lurking outside your home). This will take some consideration on your part.

Photo Courtesy of Melissa Owens

The following are some basic steps to use during training:

1. Include everyone in the home in the Dalmatian's training. The puppy must learn to listen to everyone in the household and not just one or two people. A set training schedule may only involve a couple of people in the beginning, especially if you have children. There should always be an adult present when training, but including a child will help reinforce the idea that the puppy must listen to everyone in the house. It is also an effective way for a parent to monitor a child's interaction with the puppy so that everyone plays in a way that is safe and follows the rules.

2. To get started, select an area where you and your puppy have no other distractions, including noise. Leave your phone and other devices out of range so that you are able to keep your attention on the puppy.

3. Stay happy and excited about the training. Your puppy will pick up on your enthusiasm and will focus better because of it.

4. Be consistent and firm as you teach.

5. Bring special treats to the first few training sessions, such as pieces of chicken or small treats.

Sit

Start to teach the command "Sit" when your puppy is around eight weeks old.

Once you settle into your quiet training location:

1. Hold out a treat.
2. Move the treat over your puppy's head. This will make the puppy move back.
3. Say, "Sit," as the puppy's haunches touch the floor.

Having a second person around to demonstrate this with your puppy will be helpful, as the person can sit to show the dog what you mean.

Wait until your puppy starts to sit down and say, "Sit" as he sits. If your puppy finishes sitting down, give praise. Naturally, this will make your puppy excited and wiggly, so it may take a bit of time before he will want to sit again. When your puppy calms down, repeat the process.

It's going to take more than a couple of sessions for the puppy to fully connect your words with actions. Commands are something completely new to your little companion. Once your puppy has demonstrated mastery of the command "Sit," start teaching "Down."

Down

Repeat the same process when teaching this command as you did for Sit:

1. Tell your dog to Sit.
2. Hold out the treat.
3. Lower the treat to the floor with your dog sniffing at it. Allow your pup to lick the treat, but if he stands up, start over.
4. Say "Down" as the puppy's elbows touch the floor (make sure to say it as he does the action to help him associate the word with the action), then give praise while rewarding your puppy with the treat.

It will probably take a little less time to teach this command. Wait until your puppy has mastered "Down" before moving on to "Stay."

Stay

"Stay" is a vital command to teach because it can keep your puppy from running across a street or from running at someone who is nervous or scared of dogs. It is important your dog has mastered Sit and Down before you teach Stay. Learning this command is going to be more difficult since it is not something your puppy does naturally.

Be prepared for this command to take a bit longer to teach:

1. Tell your puppy to either Sit or Stay.
2. As you do this, place your hand in front of the puppy's face.
3. Wait until the puppy stops trying to lick your hand before you continue.
4. When the puppy settles down, take a step away. If your puppy is not moving, say, "Stay," and give a treat and some praise.

Giving your puppy the reward indicates the command is over, but you also need to indicate the command is complete. The puppy has to learn to stay until you say it is okay to leave the spot. Once you give the okay to move, do not give treats. The command "Come" should not be used as the okay word, as it is a command used for something else.

Repeat these steps, taking more steps farther away from the puppy after a successful command.

Once your puppy understands Stay when you move away, start training him to stay even if you are not moving. Extend the amount of time required for the puppy to stay in one spot so that he understands Stay ends with the "Okay" command.

When you feel that your puppy has Stay mastered, start training the puppy to "Come."

Come

This is a command you can't teach until the puppy has learned the previous commands. Before you start the training session, decide if you want to use "Come" or "Come Here." Be consistent in the words you use.

This command is important for the same reason as the previous one; if you are around people who are nervous around dogs, or if you encounter a wild animal or other distraction, this command will snap your puppy's attention back to you:

1. Leash the puppy.
2. Tell the puppy to Stay.
3. Move away from the puppy.
4. Say the command you will use for Come, and give a gentle tug on the leash toward you.

Repeat these steps, building a larger distance between you and the puppy. Once the puppy seems to understand, remove the leash, and start at a close distance. If your puppy doesn't seem to understand the command, give some visual clues about what you want. For example, you can pat your leg or snap your fingers. As soon as your puppy comes running over to you, offer a reward.

Leave It

This is a difficult training command, but you need to train your dog to "Leave It" for when you are out on a walk and want him to ignore other people or dogs.

1. Let your dog see that you have treats in your hand, then close your hand. Your fist should be close enough for your dog to sniff the treat.

143

2. Say, "Leave it," when your dog starts to sniff your hand.
3. Say, "Yes," and give your dog a treat when he turns his head away from the treats. Initially, this will probably take a while, as your dog will want those treats. Don't continue to say "Leave it," as your dog should not be learning that you will give a command more than once. You want him to learn he must do what you say the first time, which is why treats are recommended in the beginning. If a minute or more passes after giving the command, you can then issue it again, but make sure your canine is focused on you and not distracted.

These sessions should only last about five minutes. Your dog will need time to learn this command as you are teaching him to ignore something he naturally wants. When he looks away and stops sniffing when you say, "Leave it," you can move on to more advanced versions of the training:

1. Leave your hand open so that your dog can see the treats.
2. Say, "Leave it," when your dog starts to show interest. This will probably be immediate since your hand will be open, so be prepared.
    a. Close your fist if your dog continues to sniff or gets near the treats in your hand.
    b. Give your dog a treat from your other hand if he stops.

Repeat these steps until your dog finally stops trying to sniff the treats. When your dog seems to have learned this command, move on to the most difficult version of this command.

1. Place treats on the ground, or let your dog see you hide them. Then stay close to those treats.
2. Say "Leave it" when your dog starts to show interest in sniffing the treats.
    a. Place a hand over the treats if he doesn't listen.
    b. Give a treat if your dog does listen.

From here, you can start training while standing farther from the treat with your dog leashed so you can stop him if needed. Then start to use other things that your dog loves, such as a favorite toy or another tempting treat that you don't usually give him.

Drop It

This is going to be one of the most difficult commands to teach because it goes against both your puppy's instincts and interests. Your puppy wants to keep whatever he has, so you are going to have to offer him something better instead. It is essential to teach the command early, as your Dalmatian could be very destructive in the early days. Furthermore, this command could save your pooch's life. When you are out for a walk, he will probably lunge at objects that look like food. However, once he has mastered this command, he will drop anything he picks up.

Start with a toy and a large treat that your dog cannot eat in a matter of seconds, such as a rawhide. Make sure the treat you have is one your puppy does not get very often so that there is motivation to drop the toy or big treat.

1. Give your puppy the toy or large treat. If you want to use a clicker, too, pair it with the exciting treat you will use to help convince your puppy to drop the treat.
2. Show your puppy the exciting treat.
3. Say, "Drop it," and when he drops the treat or toy, tell him, "Good," and hand over the exciting treat while picking up the dropped item.
4. Repeat this immediately after your puppy finishes eating the exciting treat.

You will need to keep reinforcing this command for months after it is learned because it is not a natural instinct.

Heel

"Heel" is a command that is incredibly beneficial. It keeps your dog from weaving in front of you on a walk, potentially being a tripping hazard, and gives you a command that will help to distract your dog if a squirrel or other small animal crosses your path. Telling your dog to "heel" if you see the squirrel first can be a good reminder to your dog not to chase the squirrel.

Equally important, "heel" is a command that you need to use when socializing your dog. Your Dalmatian should know how to heel before you really start socializing him to ensure that your dog is calmer or at least is still listening to you when you approach other people and dogs.

The purpose of this command is to teach your dog to walk by your side. This can be incredibly frustrating and annoying in practice, which is what really leads to people failing to teach this command. When we go outside, we get distracted, or we just want to hurry and get back inside—especially if it is cold, hot, or raining. Failing to be consistent with this command will undermine your efforts to actually teach it. Training in all of the other commands will help you to learn your dog's personality, what works, and the rewards that will keep your Dalmatian's attention during training to "heel."

Have some of your dog's favorite treats in a small bag that you can quickly and easily access. Cut the treats down to a small size (about the size of a penny) because you are going to be giving a lot of these in the early days.

Training will begin inside. This means you will probably want to leash your dog inside, which can lead to excitement if your dog thinks you are going outside. If that happens, calm your dog before you start training. Choose the room with the most space for walking around; halls can be a good choice since there is typically ample room for walking in a straight line, which will be more like walking outside.

1. Determine which side you want your dog to walk on, then hold a treat up to your chest on the side where you want the dog so that your dog cannot reach it. This will help your dog focus on listening

to your commands. The side you choose should be the side where you want your dog to walk when you go outside; usually, people train dogs to walk on their left side, but choose the side that is most comfortable for you.

2. Point to the side you prefer, and call the dog's name; then say the word "Heel."
3. Give your puppy a treat as soon as he reaches the correct side and say "yes" or "good." If you also plan to use a clicker, use it as you give your dog the treat. Having the treat on the same side as your dog will keep him from crossing to the wrong side.
4. Move away from your dog, point to the same side, call his name, and say, "Heel."
5. Immediately reward him for coming and standing on the correct side.

Over the next few days, as your dog starts to understand what you want him to do without treats, you can start trying to throw him off by zigzagging or turning to teach him to keep you as a point of reference. When he gets the concept and remains on the correct side, start getting his attention by saying, "Look," and making eye contact. This reinforces that his attention needs to be on you and on staying by your side.

Once your dog is able to do this inside, you can start working on Heel when you are outside. You want to make sure that your dog understands the command before going outside, where there are so many distractions. If your dog is accustomed to being on one side when walking, it will be more automatic, which will go a long way toward helping him stay focused when you move from the controlled home environment to the more chaotic outdoors.

You will need to keep reinforcing this command for months after it is learned because it is not a natural instinct.

Off

This is different from training your dog not to jump on people (Chapter 9). This command is specifically to get your dog off furniture or

surfaces that may be dangerous. If your furniture has enough space for your dog, you may
not need to train for this one until a bit later.
Master the other commands first, then start
on this one as practice for when you and your
dog go somewhere else and you need him to
refrain from using other people's furniture.

This is training you will need to do on the
fly because you are training your dog to stop
an action. This means you have to react to that
undesirable action. Having treats on hand will
be essential when you see your dog getting up
on things you don't want him to be on:

1. Wait for your dog to put his paws on
   something you don't want him on.
2. Say, "Off," and lure him away with a treat
   that you keep just out of his reach.
3. Say, "Yes," and give him a treat as soon as his paws are off the
   surface.

Repeat this every time you see the behavior. It will probably take
at least half a dozen times before your dog understands he should not
perform the action anymore. Over time, switch from treats to praise or
playing with a toy.

Quiet

Besides making sure that your Dalmatian
is tired and not left at home for long stretches
of time alone, you can train your dog not to
bark out of boredom. This could prove to be a
bit of a challenge early on, as he probably isn't
going to be that vocal when you are around. If
you notice that your dog is barking more or if

your neighbors complain that your dog is really noisy when you are away, you may want to train him to be quiet.

Initially, you can use treats sparingly to reinforce quiet if your pup enjoys making noise:

1. When your puppy barks for no obvious reason, tell him to be quiet and place a treat nearby. It is almost guaranteed your dog will fall silent to sniff the treat.
2. If your dog does fall silent, say, "Good dog" or "Good quiet."

Where to Go from Here

Dalmatians are a breed that should definitely be enrolled in training courses. It helps to tire them out while giving you help in learning how to train. Unless you are a very experienced trainer, courses are strongly recommended. Keep in mind that they also provide a way to socialize, so it isn't just about training but about introducing your Dalmatian to other dogs in a more controlled environment.

*Photo Courtesy of
Sara Radtke & Brian Fijal*

Chapter 13 provides alternatives for helping your dog use up all of his energy, but you need to at least ensure that your dog learns the basic commands. The following classes can help you learn to keep calm so that your training is effective. These classes are really as much for you as they are for your dog.

Puppy Classes

> 66
>
> *Take classes, lots and lots of different classes. The Dalmatian will be around dogs (usually well-behaved dogs) that won't be in his face, making him nervous. If a classmate's dog would like to play, introduce them gently. Dogs need to get out and about a lot to feel comfortable in all settings.*
>
> CAROL CHASE HEALY
> *Fiacre Dalmatians and Parson Russell Terriers*
>
> 99

Puppies can begin to go to puppy school as early as six weeks, but you will probably want to wait until your Dalmatian has had all of his shots. You will need to set aside an hour or two so that you can research schools near you. Make sure to take the time to read the reviews and see if you can talk to people who have used a particular school or trainer. Trainers should be willing to take the time to talk to you and answer questions as well, so try talking to the people running the school. This is the beginning of obedience training, but you need to be careful around other dogs until your puppy has completed his vaccinations. Talk with your vet about when is an appropriate time to begin classes. Your vet may also be able to recommend good puppy training classes in your area.

The primary purpose of these classes is socialization. Studies show one-third of all puppies have minimal exposure to unfamiliar people and dogs during the first 20 weeks of their life. This can make the outside world pretty scary! The puppy classes give you and your puppy a

Photo Courtesy of Hannah Haeckel

chance to learn how to meet and greet other people and dogs in a controlled environment. Dogs that attend these classes are much friendlier and are less stressed about such things as large trucks, thunder, loud noises, and unfamiliar visitors. They are also less likely to be nervous or suffer from separation anxiety, a likely issue for a Dalmatian.

Puppy classes are also great training for you! The same studies show owners who attend classes learn to react appropriately when a puppy is disobedient or misbehaves. The classes teach you how to train your puppy and how to deal with the emerging headstrong nature of your dog.

Many classes will help you with some of the basic commands, like Sit and Down. Look for a class that also focuses on socialization so that your puppy can get the most out of the instruction.

Obedience Training

> *Dalmatians don't like to be told what to do, so you need to be positive when training. If it's a game, they will partake. They don't like boring, regimented training. Make it fun, make it fast, and Dalmatians will love it.*
>
> CAROL CHASE HEALY
> *Fiacre Dalmatians and Parson Russell Terriers*

Photo Courtesy of Alison Singleton

Photo Courtesy of Jasmine Baxter

After your puppy graduates from puppy school and understands most of the basic commands, you can switch to obedience classes. Some trainers offer at-home obedience training, but if you do this, it's still a good idea to also set aside regular time to socialize your pup at a dog park. If your Dalmatian attends puppy classes, the trainers there can recommend classes at the next level of training. Dogs of nearly any age can attend obedience training classes, although your dog should be old enough to listen to commands before instruction begins.

Obedience training usually includes the following:

- Teaching or reinforcing basic commands, like Sit, Stay, Come, and Down
- How to walk without pulling on the leash
- How to properly greet people and dogs, including not jumping on them

Photo Courtesy of Briana Martim

Obedience school helps you learn how to train your puppy while teaching your dog basic commands and how to behave for basic tasks, like greeting and walking. Classes usually last between seven and 10 weeks.

Ask your vet for recommendations and also consider the following when evaluating trainers:

- Are they certified, particularly the CPDT-KA certification?
- How many years have they been training dogs?
- Do they have experience with training Dalmatians?

Can you participate in the training? If the answer is no, do not use that trainer. You have to be a part of your dog's training because the trainer won't be around for most of your dog's life. Therefore, your dog has to learn to listen to you.

Photo Courtesy of Abbey Hitchcock

If your Dalmatian has anxiety, depression, or other serious behavioral problems, you need to hire a trainer to help your dog work through those issues. Do your research to be sure your trainer is an expert—preferably one with experience training intelligent, strong-willed dogs.

CHAPTER 12

Socialization

> "
>
> *Start a puppy kindergarten class as early as possible. If Dalmatians aren't made to be in the presence of other dogs from early on, there could be a problem. I don't agree with the school of thought that a pup needs to have all his shots before he can leave the house. By then the window of opportunity for great socialization has passed. You can take him to many places where there are chances to interact with people and see other dogs. He can ride around in a shopping cart at many locations and experience different sights and smells.*
>
> BARBARA ALLISON
> *Rim Rock Dalmatians*
>
> "

While they tend to be happy and goofy, you will need to teach your Dalmatian that it's all right for people and other dogs to come into your home. This is to combat their territorial instincts. To do this, you will need to invite people over to meet your dog. When a Dalmatian is young, this can make it very easy to socialize your dog with others.

Breeders tend to spend a good bit of time socializing their Dalmatian puppies, so they should have a fairly good baseline when they arrive at your house. A lot of breeders strongly recommend that puppies be taken to obedience training, not just for the training but the socialization.

Another benefit of early socialization is that it can make life much more enjoyable for everyone involved, no matter what the situation. A socialized dog will approach the world from a much better place.

Whether it is their high energy levels, their singular appearance, or something else, studies have indicated that other breeds tend to be more cautious around Dalmatians. This means that your dog may not initially be the problem. If another dog demonstrates issues with your Dalmatian, you will want to remove your

Photo Courtesy of
Louise Purrazzella

Dalmatian from the situation before he gets the wrong idea about other breeds. At the same time, when Dalmatians meet out in the world, they tend to be more excited to see one of their own, a funny little quirk about a breed that sometimes faces a bit of ostracization from other dogs.

Greeting New People

> "
> *Dalmatians have a natural tendency to guard. One of their historical uses was to guard the carriage and passengers during travel. To combat this, Dalmatians benefit from robust and ongoing socialization. Getting your Dalmatian puppy out to different places, around different people and dogs, with different sights and sounds will set him up to be a stable, confident, and well-adjusted dog.*
>
> HEATHER PARSONS
> *Bedlam Acres Dalmatians*
> "

Puppies will likely enjoy meeting new people, so make sure to invite friends over to help socialize your new canine family member. Your Dalmatian may initially react by barking, but this likely will stop as soon

Photo Courtesy of
Heather Parsons

as the person tries to pet your pooch. Still, you will need to be careful to make sure that there are no territorial behaviors.

The following is a list of methods to use when introducing your puppy to a new person:

- Try to have your puppy meet new people daily, if possible. This could be during walks or while you are doing other activities, both inside and outside of the house. If you can't meet new people daily, try to do so at least four times a week.
- Invite friends and family over and let them spend a few minutes giving the puppy their undivided attention. If your puppy has a favorite game or activity, let people know so they can play with him. This will win the little guy over very quickly and teach him new people are fun and safe to be around.
- Once your puppy is old enough to learn to do tricks (after the first month), have him perform his tricks for visitors.
- Avoid crowds for the first few months. When your puppy is older, attend dog-friendly events so he can learn to be comfortable around large groups of people.

Greeting New Dogs

> *Take your puppy to puppy and obedience classes to meet his fellow canines. You can also socialize him with dogs owned by your friends or neighbors. Stay away from dog parks unless you know the dogs there. Too many times puppies get attacked by aggressive dogs and it not only can physically hurt them, but it mentally scars them and they become dog-aggressive themselves.*
>
> DEBBIE BENNETT
> *Westview Dalmatians*

Chapter 8 explained how to introduce your new Dalmatian to your other dogs. However, meeting dogs that are not part of your household is a little different, especially since you may encounter them at any time when you are out walking. The goal is to be able to walk around your neighborhood and have your dog remain calm, refraining from running up to other dogs that may not be as friendly.

Most dogs will bow and sniff each other during an introduction. Remember to watch for signs of aggression (Chapter 8), such as raised hackles and bared teeth. It is unlikely, but it is best to be safe. Bowing, high tail, and perked ears usually mean that your Dalmatian is excited about meeting the other dog. If your Dalmatian is making noises, make sure that the sounds are playful by paying attention to the physical reaction. This applies more if you have adopted an adult, but it is always a good idea to keep an eye out for these signs, regardless of the age of your dog.

Photo Courtesy of Amanda Helvey

The best way to help a Dalmatian feel comfortable around unfamiliar dogs is to set up playdates with other dogs in a neutral place. This should make the whole experience much easier. If you have friends with dogs that are known to be very friendly, see if they are willing to have your dogs meet and play.

Don't let your Dalmatian jump up on other dogs, no matter how excited he is. This action can become a way of showing dominance, which you really don't want with your puppy, even if it is just play in the beginning. If he does jump up, immediately say, "No," to let him know it is not acceptable behavior.

The Importance of Continuing Socialization

> 66
>
> *Do it early and often! Don't stop socialization after one course of puppy training or even after one year of age. Keep doing it for at least two years! And then do it again! Dalmatians love to play with other dogs, but they need to meet a wide variety of new dogs while the window of learning is open. Just having several dogs in your own house won't do the trick. Dalmatians need to meet dogs of all sizes, colors, and fur lengths before they are one year old.*
>
> SARAH GROTE, DVM
> *Willing Hearts Dalmatian Rescue*
>
> 99

Even friendly dogs need socialization. When family and friends visit, encourage them to bring their dogs. This will remind your Dalmatian his home is a welcoming place and not somewhere he needs to exert his dominance. You do not want your pup to think he can be a terror in his own house.

You will want to do some of the early activities fairly early in your dog's life so that he has exposure to a wider range of environments, sounds,

Photo Courtesy of
Lexi Simpson

smells, and experiences. For example, if you want to bike with your dog, expose your dog to bikes so that the bike becomes a normal item.

Socializing an Adult Dog

There's no guarantee that your dog will be happy being around other dogs. You may be lucky enough to get an adult that is already well-socialized. That does not mean you can remain entirely relaxed! Your new dog may have had a terrible experience with a particular breed of dog that no one knows about, and this can result in a bad situation. You will need to be more careful with male Dalmatians meeting other male dogs because they do have a tendency to be protective around other males.

Photo Courtesy of Tracey McKenna

Your dog should be adept at the following commands before you work on socialization:

- Sit
- Down
- Stay
- Heel

"Heel" and "Stay" are especially important because they demonstrate that your dog has self-control by remaining in one place based on your command. This will be helpful when socializing because using this command will allow you to control your Dalmatian in any situation. When you go outside, you will need to be very aware of your surroundings and be able to command your dog before another dog or person gets near you.

- Use a short leash on walks. Being aware of your surroundings will start to cue you in to what is making your dog react so that you can start training him not to react negatively.
- Change direction if you notice your Dalmatian is not reacting well to a person or dog that is approaching. Avoidance is a good short-term solution until you know your dog is more accepting of the presence of other dogs or people.
- If you are not able to take a different direction, tell your dog to sit, then block

HELPFUL TIP
Aggression

Dalmatians tend to be timid if not properly socialized, and their high energy levels can be off-putting to other dogs. However, most Dalmatians are non-aggressive and make excellent family dogs with adequate and early socialization. Aggressive behavior in Dalmatians is frequently due to previous mistreatment or irresponsible breeding.

Photo Courtesy of
Sara Kane
KanePhotographyLLC

his view. This can prove to be particularly challenging, as he will try to look around from behind you. Continue to distract your dog so he will listen to you, taking his mind off what is coming toward him.

- Ask friends with friendly dogs to visit you, then meet in an enclosed space. Having one or two friendly dogs to interact with can help your Dalmatian realize not all dogs are dangerous or need to be put in their place. When dogs wander around the area together, with no real interaction, your dog will learn that the others are enjoying the outside too. So, there is no reason to try to bully them!
- Get special treats for when you go walking. At the first snarl or sign of aggression, engage the training mentality and draw upon your dog's desire for those special treats. This method is slow, but it is reliable because your dog will learn that the appearance of strangers and other dogs means special treats for him. He will realize going on a walk is a positive experience. Nonetheless, this does not train him to interact with those dogs. Combine this tip with the previous suggestion to get the best results.

Photo Courtesy of
Diane Mercado

If you have ongoing problems with your adult dog, consult a behaviorist or specialized trainer. It might be that you should keep your dog home all the time, in which case you are going to need a big yard to ensure your dog stays healthy. It's never worth the risk of having your Dalmatian around other dogs if your dog doesn't like his peers. But an expert may be able to help you so that you and your dog don't have to live a hermit-like lifestyle.

CHAPTER 13

Playtime and Exercise

Although energy levels vary between dogs and different lines, most Dalmatians could be described as medium-high energy. Some Dalmatians will be content with a daily on-leash walk, but many will require more significant exercise. Dals make great running partners. Their endurance is outstanding. They love to run and thrive with safe off-leash opportunities. Dalmatians are incredibly versatile. They excel at many different sports and events. They are a clever breed that is eager to learn. They benefit from regular training to exercise their minds as well as their bodies.

HEATHER PARSONS
Bedlam Acres Dalmatians

D almatians have lots of energy to spare, and there is little that they love more than playing with their people (with food being a pretty close second). It is incredibly easy to interact with Dalmatians and to tire them out because they are up for almost any kind of activity, as long as they are with you.

It is important to remember that your vet will need to clear your young Dalmatian before you start doing activities that include sustained running or jogging. The dog's bones and joints need to finish growing before you put that kind of strain on them. Since you will need to do a good bit of training in the early days, you should have more than enough

Photo Courtesy of
Kara Whittaker

activities to keep your Dalmatian happily entertained so that he gets both physically and mentally tired without the jogging and running. It's much easier to tire a five-month-old Dalmatian than a five-year-old Dalmatian.

Dalmatians love all kinds of activities—swimming, hiking, long walks, exploring trails, or sniffing along the beach. When your active day is over, they make fantastic cuddle buddies as you relax. Conversely, when you own a Dalmatian, you also really can't afford to take a day off from exercising because your dog is absolutely going to need daily activity. That isn't going to be difficult if you have a sizable yard where your dog can romp with you on days you don't want to go anywhere.

There are a number of positives for your dog when you ensure he gets regular exercise sessions.

- It helps keep your dog at a healthier weight.
- He will be tired enough not to be too much trouble, especially if you need to leave him alone for a little while.
- Exercise is a great time to bond with your Dalmatian.

166

Exercise Needs

> *Dalmatians will exercise as much as you allow them to, and they will demand the amount of exercise that they have become accustomed to. If your dog runs 10 miles a day, then he will want and need to run 10 miles a day. Dalmatians do require a decent amount of exercise (at least one to two hours a day) to remain healthy, so don't let your dog become sedentary. Mental stimulation is extremely important. Puzzle games and other toys are great. If given nothing to do, Dalmatians will entertain themselves, sometimes by digging, chewing, or other destructive behavior.*
>
> CARLA WAYMAN
> *Spotted Way Dalmatians*

Photo Courtesy of Gitana Dainauskas

Exercising a Dalmatian is a serious responsibility. Your Dalmatian will need close to two hours a day until he reaches his senior years (Chapter 18). It's perfectly fine to break that up over the course of the day, with one vigorous 45-minute to hour-long exercise session, then several walks and training sessions to round out the rest of the time. On weekends and vacation days, you can spend a lot more time out-of-doors having fun.

If your Dalmatian is not getting enough activity, it will probably be very obvious. He will take out his energy and boredom on your furniture, doors, and home when he is still young. When he is a mature adult, it will not be so obvious unless you are checking his weight regularly. It can get dangerous if you don't meet a Dalmatian's exercise needs because being overweight will increase the potential for a lot of ailments, especially as your dog ages.

If you have a puppy, frequent 10-to-15-minute training sessions can be the activity as well. Short walks can double as training sessions. You can try "Sit" and "Heel" during walks once your dog reaches a stage where he is able to do these commands well in your home.

You will have limits about how much cold and rainy weather you can handle. This doesn't mean that your Dalmatian can skip being active—not if you don't want your dog to take it out around your home. Fortunately, there are plenty of indoor activities that you can do on days when going outside really isn't such a good idea.

Outdoor Activities

> Dalmatians are true jacks-of-all-trades. They have a keen sense of smell and compete at the top levels of scentwork. They are great partners for rally and obedience. Many Dals love to swim, and their athletic build makes them fantastic dock divers. Their natural athleticism makes them a great fit for agility. Dalmatians are very powerful and can pull impressive weights in weight-pull competitions. Their endurance makes them perfect mushing partners for bikejoring, sledding, or canicross. They have a strong prey drive, which can be seen in their impressive times for coursing ability tests.
>
> HEATHER PARSONS
> *Bedlam Acres Dalmatians*

Photo Courtesy of Ashleigh Boyd

The possibilities are pretty much endless in terms of what your Dalmatian can do outside. If you live in an area with snow, he will be the perfect companion for kids playing in the snow or going out to do chores and other activities in the cold. If you live near woods, your Dalmatian will love exploring and hiking around the area. If you live in a city or suburban area, your Dalmatian can join you for jogs and bike rides. If you want to be outside, you have a dog who can join you for pretty much everything except rock climbing.

Since this is a thin, short-haired breed, if you are going outside during winter and it is cold or snowy, you may need to put a coat on your Dalmatian if you plan to be out for more than 30 minutes. You don't have to worry so much about overheating, especially if water is involved in your activities, but this is a breed that does need some extra warmth when it is cold. They aren't built for the cold, but they can enjoy it just as much as you if you bundle them up before engaging in winter fun.

If you plan to spend a day outside being active, especially when it gets warmer, make sure to bring water for your Dalmatian. They may not be prone to overheating, but Dalmatians do need to drink a lot over the course of an active day.

> **"**
>
> *Walk your dog in different places like parks, shopping malls, downtown, or around the airport. Give him lots of different sights and sounds to become accustomed to. Take lots of training classes to develop his mind and help him learn to love training. Once your dog has an excellent recall, take him on hikes in hills, mountains, or beaches, and you'll both benefit.*
>
> CAROL CHASE HEALY
> *Fiacre Dalmatians and Parson Russell Terriers*
>
> **"**

Treasure Hunting

> **"**
>
> *What Dalmatians can excel at is only limited by owners' training ability! They absolutely love to chase the plastic bunny in coursing events. They do really well in nosework and agility, too. They are naturals at coaching and seem to do well with horses. They are also good vermin dogs around the farm. Many have a very high prey drive, so they will need to be trained from a young age that chickens are not to be killed but mice and rats are fair game.*
>
> BARBARA ALLISON
> *Rim Rock Dalmatians*
>
> **"**

Dalmatians have a lot of skills, and you can really encourage your dog to explore those skills by conducting treasure hunts. In addition to tiring out your canine, these can help keep him feeling mentally stimulated and happy. The fact that it means getting a bit more praise will be the icing on the cake as far as your dog is concerned.

1. Establish what you want the treasure to be. It should be something that your dog doesn't get often. Treats are usually the go-to because they provide something with a smell he will want. You can buy something special, or you can make a special treat to really get your dog excited.
2. For the first round, let your dog watch you hide the treat. This is how you introduce your dog to the idea that you will put something out of sight and that you want him to retrieve it. You will probably need to do this several times, so if you use treats, give him smaller pieces instead of a full, large treat during the learning process. Change where you "hide" the treat so that your dog understands that it isn't always in the same place.
3. When you feel that your dog understands what you want him to do, tell your good boy to "Stay" (or if you haven't gotten that far in

training, have someone hold your dog), then go hide the treat someplace. Over time, you actually hide treats in multiple locations to really challenge your dog's abilities to sniff out where the goodies are. Return to your dog and let him go hunting. When he finds a treat, be effusive in your praise to let him know he's doing it right.

A treat with a lot of praise? Yeah, this can easily be one of your dog's favorite games really quickly. It's also something you can play inside, though you may want to use dry treats instead of something that could get ground into your furniture, carpet, or other items.

FUN FACT
Firehouse Dogs

Dalmatians have a long history as firehouse companions. Initially, Dalmatians could often be seen running alongside horse-drawn fire engines. These dogs served two purposes: alerting the public of the approaching fire engine by barking and serving as guard dogs to the horses. By the time horse-drawn fire engines were replaced by automobiles, Dalmatians had cemented their place as firefighters' canine companions.

Course/Lure Training

> 66
>
> Nosework for our Dalmatians is their forte! They are also incredibly fast, so enjoy lure coursing ability tests. The right Dalmatian can excel at any sport with the right training and guidance.
>
> MICHELLE POTTER
> *Symphony Dalmatians*
> 99

Depending on where you live, this may be called either course or lure training. The activity involves your dog chasing after something moving quickly. Since Dalmatians have been used as hunters, this gives them some outlet for doing what comes naturally to them—chasing. Unlike hunting, though, the lures are just fake animals that look realistic and move on a mechanism to stay ahead of the dogs. The lures are able to quickly change direction, giving the dogs a real run for their money. You can probably find some lure clubs in your area.

Like agility training, your dog needs to go to the vet to ensure a clean bill of health before starting on lure training.

Photo Courtesy of Dacia DeVinney

Fetch and Frisbee

> *Exercise is important for Dalmatians. Physical exercise comes in many forms, including long walks, running with their owner, chasing balls, playing with other dogs at the dog park, and running alongside horses as they did for centuries. Keeping it new and fresh will keep them mentally sharp. Toys meant to make them think will keep them from getting bored as well.*
>
> EMILY HUF
> *Dream Chaser Dalmatians*

Since teeth issues are a potential problem for Dalmatians, you will want to use something soft for this game. There are plenty of great discs you can use that won't harm your dog's mouth. A soft disc usually runs between $5 and $20, so it won't be a major investment.

All you have to do is throw the disc, and your dog will get it. Training your dog to bring it back is going to be the trick, but given how much fun this game is likely to be with your dog, it shouldn't be too hard. Just

*Photo Courtesy of
Billy Swift*

add "Fetch" to your training, and your dog will be more than happy with the results.

Keep in mind this is a very drooly dog, so it won't take long before those discs are slimy when you play. Also, those teeth are probably going to do some damage to the discs. If your dog enjoys the game, it won't hurt to get a stash of discs so that you don't run out of them. When you play, take a couple of discs with you so that you can rotate which one you are throwing to reduce the amount of drool you have to deal with.

A Jogger's or Biker's Best Companion

> **"**
>
> *Dalmatians are great runners and they have a natural 'coaching' instinct. Dalmatians were bred for hundreds of years to run along-side horses and carriages, and they still have that instinct, much like a Pointer instinctively points at birds. If you start jogging, your Dalmatian will instinctively 'coach' alongside or in front of you. The same goes for riding ATVs or riding horses. They love running with things.*
>
> RACHEL T.
> *The Spotted Dog Minnesota Dalmatians*
>
> **"**

Dalmatians are among the best canine jogging companions. Perhaps the only real downside is that when you are done, your Dalmatian may still have some energy to spare. Ending a jogging session with a nice romp through a sprinkler or playing a game of fetch can help burn off the rest of your pup's energy without having to consume a lot more of your own.

If you prefer to ride a bike, you will need to train your Dalmatian how to run next to a bike before taking any long trips, but this probably won't take your dog too long to learn.

Hiking and Backpacking

If you love being out in nature, this is a great dog to take hiking and backpacking. Dalmatians can easily keep up with you, and they will enjoy the sights as much as you (and the smells a lot more). They are made for being out and getting time in the woods, mountains, and forests.

Swimming

> *Dalmatians can enjoy a variety of outdoor activities. This includes agility, hiking, walks, swimming, running, and playing with other dogs, as well as playing with toys.*
>
> FANNY FIDDLER
> *North Paw Dalmatians*

Dalmatians only have one short coat, which doesn't interfere with swimming. Also, they have webbed feet. This is a dog that can keep up with you in the pool or a natural body of water. However, they do need to be introduced to swimming early in life.

Start your Dalmatian in pools, ponds, and smaller lakes. Shallower depths can help your dog feel safer faster. Don't worry—you don't have to teach your dog to swim. Any initial apprehension will give way to those well-honed instincts, and your dog will soon be swimming much faster than any human, usually by the end of the first swim. Still, stay in shallower locations for at least the first few swims.

Photo Courtesy of Jenna Coutinho

Once your dog is happy and excited about water, you can move on to deeper water. Just make sure that you stay close by and always keep an eye on your dog. Your Dalmatian may overdo swimming in the beginning, then not have enough energy to return to shore. If you go to an ocean or other large body of water, consider a life vest for your dog but also remain vigilant.

Traveling

Your Dalmatian will *love* to see new places, experience new smells, and see the sights and sounds wherever you go.

Make sure to travel with water so that your dog doesn't get dehydrated. You'll want to ensure that the car ride is as comfortable and safe as possible. It is best to have your dog in a crate or secured so that he doesn't fall over during sudden stops or turns.

Build in stops for pee breaks at least every four hours.

You will want to start traveling when your Dalmatian is young, such as taking him to the park, store, or other location. Once your canine is trained in all of the basic commands, you can go for longer trips.

Put Them to Work

> **❝**
>
> *Dalmatians have a retentive memory; they can remember how you respond, reward, and discipline their everyday behavior. That is why they were keen fire dogs, known for their attention to detail, or carriage dogs, decades ago, known for their speed. They have the endurance to perform athletically and serve their purpose of helping.*
>
> REBECCA BIERKO
> *Georgia Dalmatians*
>
> **❞**

Photo Courtesy of
Becky Stancik

As a jack of all trades, your Dalmatian can do pretty much any kind of work you throw at him, within reason. They can make fantastic therapy dogs with the right training. You will need to wait until your dog is a bit older and calmer, but as your Dalmatian starts to slow down, working as a therapy dog can give him the kind of attention that makes up for not being as active.

This will require a good bit of research as you will need to determine what requirements and training your dog needs prior to registering him as a therapy dog.

Indoor Activities

The real downside to having an energetic dog is that during bad weather, it is much harder to make sure he gets enough daily exercise. Here are some things you can do inside to help your dog stay healthy.

Hide-and-Seek

Hide-and-seek is a game you can play once your dog understands proper behavior in the home. Since your Dalmatian will probably hear you wherever you hide, you can also make it a game of hide the toy. If you distract your pup while someone else hides the toy, your Dalmatian will have a great time trying to locate it!

Advanced Training for Tricks

If you love doing something like yoga or martial arts, there's probably some way for your dog to join you—just don't expect to get too much done early on since your dog is going to need to understand what you are doing. In the meantime, he is going to think you are trying to play.

Puzzle Toys!

> **"**
>
> *Dalmatians are very easy to train. My dogs usually learn a command or trick within five minutes. Because they are smart, they can become bored and may lose interest, so try to keep training sessions short and interesting. Change the routine. Some Dalmatians can problem solve, so be careful when locking crates and doors, and when hiding things from them. They will watch you and learn.*
>
> CARLA WAYMAN
> *Spotted Way Dalmatians*
> **"**

Puzzle toys are a fun way to get your dog to move around without you having to do much. Most puzzle toys are food-based, so the dog will need to figure out how to get the treats out. If you use these toys, keep in mind that your dog isn't likely to work off the extra calories, and you should adjust his meals accordingly.

Cuddle Time

Younger Dalmatians aren't likely to be fans of cuddling unless they are tired—just like toddlers or small children. Once they get older and settle down, these dogs can be absolutely fantastic cuddlers because they just love being around you. As long as you make sure your Dalmatian gets enough exercise, he will be just as happy to relax at the end of the day as you are.

What to Avoid

There are a lot of things you can do to exercise a Dalmatian, but with an intelligent dog like this, you have to be very careful about not letting him get into trouble.

Overexertion in Puppies

> "
> *You don't want to overwhelm your Dalmatian puppy. Signs of puppy stress can be subtle, so if you notice your puppy yawning a lot or retreating to curl in a ball, he may be stressed and need a break.*
>
> SARAH GROTE, DVM
> *Willing Hearts Dalmatian Rescue*
> "

Dalmatian growth plates are not closed until the dog is about 18 months old. The best way to work out the energy of a Dalmatian puppy is to give him a lot of off-leash play on soft surfaces, such as lawns.

Swimming is also a great activity if you start training him early, and it won't hurt his joints.

Puppies also get tired as much by mental work as by physical activity. They don't require nearly as much activity to tire out as an adult. Let their flagging energy levels help you determine when to stop play, and be ready for them to be energetic all too soon afterward.

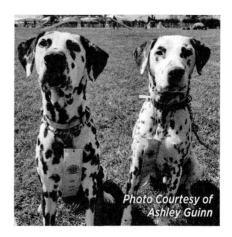

Photo Courtesy of
Ashley Guinn

Post-Meal Exercise

Unfortunately, Dalmatians are at risk of gastric dilation volvulus, better known as bloat. The ailment is covered in detail in Chapter 17, but one of the ways to increase the risk of this life-threatening problem is to exercise your dog right after eating. Give your dog at least an hour to digest his food before you do any kind of exercise; some experts recommend waiting two hours to be safe.

PART 4

Taking Care of
Your Dalmatian

CHAPTER 14

Nutrition

As a breed that falls between medium- and large-sized, you have to be careful about Dalmatian nutrition because it is a much harder balancing act as their classification depends in part on their diet. If you feed them too much, they will be classed as large dogs, but they shouldn't be. It isn't likely you will have a problem getting them to eat because these dogs love eating, even if something isn't exactly food.

Considering puppies are typically fully grown at about 16 months but are not considered mature until they are between two and two and a half years old, it is essential to ensure your high-energy puppy has the right foods to help him grow strong and healthy.

Your dog is going to want to eat as often as you are willing to feed him. Between treats for training and meals, it is very easy to overfeed Dalmatians, which can be detrimental to their health.

Why a Healthy Diet Is Important

> **❝**
>
> *It is very important to feed your Dalmatian a healthy diet. This means spending a bit more on food and ensuring the ingredients are good and not filled with fats and fillers. Most Dalmatians require a low purine diet and foods such as organ meats, lentils, peas, and Brewer's yeast should be avoided. Foods high in purines can cause urine crystals or kidney stones in this breed. Treats should also be healthy and fed only in moderation. It is important that Dalmatians get daily exercise. Ensuring you have regular visits to a veterinarian is also important in maintaining overall health.*
>
> FANNY FIDDLER
> *North Paw Dalmatians*
>
> **❞**

Dalmatians need more calories than some breeds to sustain themselves. But even if your Dalmatian is active, it doesn't mean he is burning all the calories he takes in, especially if you have an open treat policy. Just as you should not be eating all day, your puppy shouldn't be either.

You need to be aware of roughly how many calories your dog eats a day, including treats, so be mindful of your dog's weight and whether or not he is putting on pounds. This will tell you if you should adjust his food intake or change the food to something more nutritious but with fewer calories.

Always talk with your vet if you have concerns about your Dalmatian's weight.

Dangerous Foods

> 66
>
> *Foods to avoid that are high in purines are organ meats, beef, wild game meat, and some types of fish (including anything in the herring family). Yeast is also in many dog foods and is very high in purines. Treats are very often made from organ meat, so check those labels. Stay away from foods with by-product meal because that usually means organs. Also, stay away from corn, wheat, and soy, as they are unneeded fillings that will cause nothing but problems. Rice and oats are typically okay.*
>
> JENNY POTTS
>
> *Seeing Spots Dalmatians of Spokane*
>
> 99

Dogs can eat some raw meat without having to worry about the kinds of problems a person would encounter. However, there are some human foods that could be fatal to your Dalmatian, in part because the kinds of raw meat that humans offer have been treated with a range of chemicals. Raw diets will be examined later in this chapter so you can protect your Dalmatian from the potential risks associated with raw foods.

The following is a list of foods you should **NEVER** feed your dog:

- Apple seeds
- Chocolate
- Coffee
- Cooked bones (They can kill a dog when the bones splinter in the dog's mouth or stomach.)
- Corn on the cob (The cob is deadly to dogs; corn off the cob is fine.)
- Grapes/raisins
- Macadamia nuts
- Onions and chives
- Peaches, persimmons, and plums
- Tobacco (Your Dalmatian will not realize it is not a food and may eat it if it's left out.)

- Xylitol (a sugar substitute in candies and baked goods)
- Yeast

In addition to this list, consult the Canine Journal for a lengthy list of other dangerous foods. (http://www.caninejournal.com/foods-not-to-feed-dog/)

Canine Nutrition

Canines are largely carnivorous, and protein is a significant dietary need (as discussed later in this chapter). However, they need more than just protein to be healthy.

The following table provides the primary nutritional requirements for dogs:

Nutrient	Sources	Puppy	Adult
Protein	Meat, eggs, soybeans, corn, wheat, peanut butter	22.0% of diet	18.0% of diet
Fats	Fish oil, flaxseed oil, canola oil, pork fat, poultry fat, safflower oil, sunflower oil, soybean oil	8.0 to 15.0% of diet	5.0 to 15.0% of diet
Calcium	Dairy, animal organ tissue, meats, legumes (typically beans)	1.0% of diet	0.6% of diet
Phosphorus	Meat and pet supplements	0.8% of diet	0.5% of diet
Sodium	Meat, eggs	0.3% of diet	0.06% of diet

The following are the remaining nutrients dogs require, all of them less than 1% of a puppy or adult diet:

- Arginine
- Histidine
- Isoleucine
- Leucine
- Lysine
- Methionine + cystine
- Phenylalanine + tyrosine

- Threonine
- Tryptophan
- Valine
- Chloride

It is best to avoid giving your dog human foods that have a lot of sodium and preservatives. Water is also absolutely essential to keep your dog healthy. Make a habit of checking your dog's water bowl several times a day so that your dog does not get dehydrated.

Proteins and Amino Acids

> **"**
>
> *Unless specifically bred to do so, most Dalmatians do not have the ability to break down purines in their diet, resulting in a build-up of uric acid which crystalizes in the urine and can form certain types of bladder and kidney stones. New owners need to be familiar with the ingredients in commercial dog food and choose accordingly. Dalmatians should be fed a low-purine diet that is hydrated (where their bowl is filled with water and kibble) for their entire lives. This part of owning a Dalmatian is tedious and can be expensive but is not optional.*
>
> CARLA WAYMAN
> *Spotted Way Dalmatians*
>
> **"**

Since dogs are carnivores, protein is one of the most important nutrients in a healthy dog's diet. (Dogs should not eat as much meat as their close wolf relatives do. Dogs' diets and needs have changed significantly since they became human companions.) Protein contains the necessary amino acids to produce glucose, which is essential for giving your dog energy. A lack of protein in your dog's diet will result in him being lethargic. His coat may start to look dull, and he is likely to lose weight.

Conversely, if your dog gets too much protein, his body will store the excess protein as fat, and he will gain weight.

Meat is the best source of protein for your dog. If you plan to feed him a vegetarian diet, it is very important that you talk to your vet first. It is incredibly difficult to ensure that a carnivore receives adequate protein while on a vegetarian diet. Puppies, in particular, need to have adequate protein to be healthy adults, so you may need to give your puppy a diet with meat, then switch to a vegetarian diet after your Dalmatian becomes an adult.

Protein is particularly important for taking care of your Dalmatian's coat. While you don't want to be excessive, do make sure that your dog gets adequate protein every day. This will be easier if you make meals for your dog. If you don't have time, make sure to buy foods that are high in protein.

Fat and Fatty Acids

Photo Courtesy of
Jasmine Baxter

Most fats that your dog needs are found in meat. Seed oils provide a lot of the necessary healthy fats, too, with peanut butter being one of the most common sources. Fats break down into fatty acids, which your dog needs for fat-soluble vitamins that help with regular cell functions. Perhaps the most obvious benefit of fats and fatty acids can be seen in your dog's coat. Your Dalmatian's coat will look and feel much healthier when he is getting the right nutrients.

The following is a list of potential health issues that might arise if your dog does not get adequate fats in his daily diet:

- His coat will look less healthy.
- His skin may be dry and itchy.
- His immune system could be compromised, making it easier for your dog to get sick.
- He may have an increased risk of heart disease. The primary concern if your dog gets too much fat is that he will become obese, leading to additional health problems.

Photo Courtesy of Heather Baker

Carbohydrates and Cooked Foods

Dogs have been living with humans for millennia, so their dietary needs have evolved like our own. They can eat foods with carbohydrates to supplement the energy typically provided by proteins and fats. If you cook grains (such as barley, corn, and rice) prior to feeding them to your dog, it will be easier for him to digest those complex carbohydrates. Note that if your dog is allergic to grains, potatoes and sweet potatoes are also high in carbohydrates.

Different Dietary Requirements for Different Life Stages

Different stages of a dog's life have different nutritional needs.

Puppy Food

During the first 12 months of their lives, puppies' bodies are growing. To be healthy, they need more calories and have different nutritional needs to promote growth, so feed them a food made specifically for puppies. Puppies can have up to four meals a day. Just be careful not to overfeed them, particularly if you use treats during training.

Adult Dog Food

The primary difference between puppy food and adult dog food is puppy food is higher in calories and nutrients. Dog food manufacturers reduce these nutrients in adult dog food, as adults no longer need lots of calories to sustain growth. As a rule, when a canine reaches about 90% of his predicted adult size, you should switch to adult dog food.

The size of your Dalmatian and his level of activity are key in determining how much to feed him. The following table is a general recommendation for your adult Dalmatian's daily food consumption. Initially, you may want to focus on the calories as you try to find the right balance for your dog.

Dog Size	Calories per day
30 lbs.	900 during hot months 1,400 during cold months
50 lbs.	1,350 during hot months 2,000 during cold months
70 lbs.	1,680 during hot months 2,500 during cold months

To minimize the risk of bloat (covered in Chapter 17), you should feed your Dalmatian at least twice a day (rather than feeding him just one big meal), so you can divide up the calories according to this schedule. Keep in mind these recommendations are per day and not per meal. To make sure your dog feels like a real part of the family, let your pup eat when you do, even if he doesn't get that much food at a time.

It is also recommended that you set the food and water bowls at an elevated level so that your dog doesn't have to lean over so far to eat. This can help reduce the risk of bloat as well. If you notice your Dalmatian eating too quickly, consider getting a dog feeder that limits how quickly he can eat. After 15 minutes, pick up the food bowl so that he does not continuously eat over the course of the day. However, always leave fresh water out for him, making it easily accessible all day and night.

If you plan to add wet food to your dog's diet, pay attention to the total calorie intake and adjust how much you feed him between the kibble and wet food. The total calories in the kibble and wet food

Photo Courtesy of
Erin Jainnini

should balance out so as not to exceed your dog's needs. The same is true if you give a lot of treats over the course of the day. You should factor treat calories into how much you feed your dog at mealtimes.

If you feed your dog homemade food (discussed later in this chapter), you should learn your nutrition facts, and you should pay close attention to calories instead of cup measurements.

Senior Dog Food

Senior dogs are not always capable of being as active as they were in their younger days. If you notice your dog is slowing down or suffers joint pain and shows a lack of stamina when taking long walks, you can assume your Dalmatian is entering his senior years. Consult with your vet if you think it is time to change the type of food you feed your dog.

The primary difference between adult and senior dog food is senior dog food contains less fat and more antioxidants to help fight weight gain. Senior dogs also need more protein, which will probably make your dog happy because that usually means more meat. Protein helps to maintain your dog's aging muscles. He should also be eating less phosphorus during his golden years to avoid the risk of developing hyper-phosphatemia. This is a condition where dogs have excessive amounts of phosphorus in their bloodstream, and older dogs are at greater risk of developing it. The level of phosphorus in the body is controlled by the kidneys; as such, elevated levels of phosphorus are usually an indication of a problem with the kidneys.

Senior dog food has the correct number of calories for reduced activity, which means no adjustment of quantity is needed unless you notice weight gain. Consult your vet if you notice your dog is putting on weight because this could be a sign of illness.

Your Dog's Meal Options

You have three primary choices for what to feed your dog, or you can use a combination of the three, depending on your situation and your dog's specific needs.

Commercial Food

Make sure that you are buying the best dog food you can afford. Take the time to research each of your options, particularly the nutritional value of the food, and review this annually. Make sure the food you are giving your dog is high quality, and always take into account your dog's size, energy level, and age. Your puppy may not need puppy food for as long as other breeds, and dog food for seniors may not be necessary for Dalmatians. You'll need to pay attention to your dog's individual needs to determine if he needs a special food for his age.

The website Pawster provides several great articles about which commercial dog foods are best for Dalmatians. Since new foods frequently come on the market, check periodically to see if there are better foods that have become available.

If you aren't sure which brand of food is best, talk with the breeder about the foods they recommend. Breeders are really the best guides for you, as they are experts. But you can also ask your vet.

Some dogs may be picky eaters that get tired of repeatedly eating the same food. While you shouldn't frequently change the brand of food because that can upset your dog's stomach, you can get foods that have assorted flavors. You can also change the taste by adding a bit of wet (canned) food. Adding one-fourth to one-third of a can for each meal is an easy change to make to ensure your dog's happiness.

For more details on commercial options, check out the website Dog Food Advisor. It provides reviews on various dog food brands, as well as information on recalls and contamination issues.

Commercial Dry Food

Dry dog food is what most people feed their dogs.

Pros

- ⊘ Convenience
- ⊘ Variety
- ⊘ Availability
- ⊘ Affordability
- ⊘ Manufacturers follow nutritional recommendations. (Not all of them follow this, so do your brand research before you buy.)
- ⊘ Specially formulated for different canine life-stages
- ⊘ Can be used for training
- ⊘ Easy to store

Cons

- ⊗ Requires research to ensure you don't buy doggy junk food
- ⊗ Packaging is not always honest
- ⊗ Recalls for food contamination
- ⊗ Loose FDA nutritional regulations
- ⊗ Low-quality food may have questionable ingredients

The convenience and ease on your budget mean you are almost certainly going to buy kibble for your dog. This is perfectly fine, and most dogs will be more than happy to eat kibble. Be sure you know what brand you are feeding your dog, and pay attention to kibble recalls so you can stop feeding your dog a certain brand if necessary. Check out the following sites regularly for recall information:

- Dog Food Recalls – www.dogfoodadvisor.com
- American Kennel Club – www.AKC.org
- Dog Food Guide – www.dogfood.guide

Commercial Wet Food

Most dogs prefer wet dog food over kibble, but it is also more expensive. Wet dog food can be purchased in large packs that are easy to store.

Pros

- ⊘ Helps keep dogs hydrated
- ⊘ Has a richer scent and flavor
- ⊘ Easier to eat for dogs with dental problems (particularly those with missing teeth) or if a dog has been ill
- ⊘ Convenient and easy to serve
- ⊘ Unopened, it can last between one and three years
- ⊘ Balanced based on current pet nutrition recommendations

Cons

- ⊗ Dog bowls must be washed after every meal.
- ⊗ Can soften bowel movements
- ⊗ Can be messier than kibble
- ⊗ Once opened, it has a short shelf-life and should be covered and refrigerated.
- ⊗ More expensive than dry dog food and comes in small quantities
- ⊗ Packaging is not always honest.
- ⊗ Recalls for food contamination
- ⊗ Loose FDA regulations

Like dry dog food, wet dog food is convenient, and picky dogs are much more likely to eat it than kibble. If your dog gets sick, use wet dog food to ensure that he is still eating and gets the necessary nutrition each day. It may be harder to switch back to kibble once your Dalmatian is healthy, but you can always add a little wet food to make each meal more appetizing.

CELEBRITY DALMATIANS
Anheuser-Busch Dalmatian

In 1950, the world-famous Budweiser Clydesdales were assigned a Dalmatian mascot. Since then, the Anheuser-Busch horses have enjoyed a Dalmatian companion who sits beside the driver. In 2015 the newest Budweiser Dalmatian was introduced: two-month-old Barley. This lucky pup's name was selected following a Twitter poll conducted by the company.

Raw Diet

For dogs prone to food allergies, raw diets can help prevent an allergic reaction to wheat and processed foods. Raw diets are heavy in raw meats, bones, vegetables, and specific supplements. Some of the benefits of a raw diet include the following:

- Improves your dog's coat and skin
- Improves immune system
- Improves health (as a result of better digestion)
- Increases energy
- Increases muscle mass

Raw diets are meant to give your dog the kind of food canines ate before they became domesticated. It means giving your dog uncooked meats, whole (uncooked) bones, and a small amount of dairy products. It doesn't include processed food of any kind—not even food cooked in your kitchen.

There are potential risks to this diet. Dogs have been domesticated for millennia. Trying to force them to eat the kind of diet they ate hundreds of years ago does not always work as intended, primarily because dogs' digestive systems have evolved, so they process raw meat differently than they once did.

There are also many risks associated with feeding dogs uncooked meals, particularly if the food has been contaminated. Things like bacteria pose a serious risk and can be transferred to you if your dog gets sick. Many medical professionals also warn about the dangers of giving dogs bones, even if they are uncooked. Bones can splinter in your dog's mouth and puncture the esophagus or stomach.

The Canine Journal (www.caninejournal.com) provides a lot of information about a raw diet, including different recipes and how to transition your dog to this diet. Always talk to your veterinarian before putting your dog on a new kind of diet.

Homemade Diet

> **"**
>
> *Dalmatians should have a balanced diet of protein, vegetables, and fruits. We feed our Dalmatians a mix of dry dog food and our own homemade recipe. We also incorporate freshly chopped basil for our high uric acid (HUA) Dalmatian. Basil works to break up urinary stones that these Dalmatians can form. HUA Dalmatians need a diet very low in purines and lots of water.*
>
> JACLYN HESLIP
> *Moen Lake Dalmatians*
>
> **"**

The best home-cooked meals should be planned in advance so that your Dalmatian gets the correct nutritional balance. Typically, 50% of your dog's food should be animal protein (fish, poultry, and organ meats). About 25% should be complex carbohydrates. The remaining 25% should be from fruits and vegetables, particularly foods like pumpkin, apples, bananas, and green beans. These foods provide extra flavor

Photo Courtesy of
Sara Radtke & Brian Fijal

your Dalmatian will probably love while filling him up faster and reducing the chance of overeating.

The following are a few sites where you can learn how to make homemade meals for canines. They are not breed-specific, so if you have more than one dog, these meals can be made for all your furry canine friends:

- Hublore (http://hublore.blogspot.com/2011/05/homemade-dog-food-recipe.html)
- Homemade Dog Food with a Special Ingredient (https://pethelpful.com/dogs/Homemade-Dog-Food-with-an-Extra-Special-Ingredient)
- Canine Journal (https://www.caninejournal.com/homemade-dog-food-recipes/)
- DIY Homemade Dog Food (https://damndelicious.net/2015/04/27/diy-homemade-dog-food/)

Keep in mind the foods your Dalmatian absolutely should not eat. You can also mix some of the food you make for yourself into your Dalmatian's meal. Do not feed your Dalmatian from your plate! Split the food, placing your dog's meal into a bowl so that your canine understands your food is just for you.

Scheduling Meals

> *Feeding is very important. The pup needs to be fed three or four times a day depending on age. I suggest giving the pup the feed your (reputable!) breeder recommends. If the pup doesn't clean up his feed in five minutes, take it away. There is nothing fun about a finicky puppy. Teach the pup to eat when you feed him by not leaving it there all day.*
>
> BARBARA ALLISON
> *Rim Rock Dalmatians*

Your Dalmatian will probably expect you to stick to a schedule, which definitely includes mealtimes. If treats and snacks are something you establish as a normal routine, your dog will expect that too! For puppies, plan to have three or four meals, while adults and seniors should typically have two meals a day.

Food Allergies and Intolerance

Photo Courtesy of Debbie Sowul

Whenever you start your dog on a new type of food (even if it's simply a different flavor), you need to monitor him while he becomes accustomed to the change. Food allergies are fairly common in Dalmatians, and the symptoms manifest themselves as hot spots, which are similar to rashes in humans. Your dog may start scratching or chewing specific spots on his body, and his fur or hair could start falling out around those spots. Some dogs don't have individual hot spots, but the allergy shows up on their entire coat. If your Dalmatian seems to be shedding more hair than normal, take him to the vet to be checked for food allergies.

Photo Courtesy of Brian L. Smith

If you give your dog something his stomach cannot handle, it will probably be obvious when he is unable to hold his bowels. If he is already house-trained, he will probably either pant at you or whimper to let you know he needs to go outside. Get him outside as quickly as you can so that he does not have an accident. Flatulence will also probably occur more often if your Dalmatian has a food intolerance.

Since the symptoms of food allergies and intolerances look similar to a reaction to nutritional deficiencies, you should visit your vet immediately! This is especially true if you notice any problems with your dog's coat or skin.

CHAPTER 15

Grooming – Productive Bonding

Dalmatians are tricky when it comes to grooming. When they are clean, they don't require much more than regular brushing. However, this is a breed that loves to get outside and get dirty. Since they are also prone to some skin issues (covered in Chapters 16 and 17), you'll want to make grooming a regular part of your weekly activities. This is a dog that sheds a lot, so daily brushings may be the best way to cut down on the amount of fur you have flying around the house.

The problem starts to sneak in if your Dalmatian decides that bath time or other types of grooming just aren't for him. This is where you really need to have a well-trained dog because they can be quite stubborn if they decide they don't like to be groomed.

Dalmatians can be a dream when it comes to maintenance as long as you train them well. If you don't train your Dalmatian, you are in for a fight when bathing him.

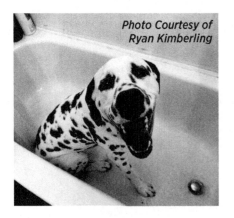
Photo Courtesy of Ryan Kimberling

Then there are the other regular grooming tasks, such as brushing your dog's teeth and trimming his nails. If you find that you simply can't get your Dalmatian to sit still for a nail clipping, or if your Dalmatian has a blood disorder (covered in Chapter 17), it is best to pay a professional to take care of those nails.

Grooming Focus and Tools

> "
>
> *Dalmatians require few baths per year and no haircuts. They are very good at keeping themselves clean and, after a bath or swimming, do not have that 'wet dog smell' we're all familiar with. Dalmatians do, however, shed—a lot. Daily brushing can help. I prefer to use a vacuum on mine as it seems to get rid of most of the loose hair. One thing every Dalmatian owner should know is that they have very stiff and short hairs that cling to everything and are hard to get off most fabrics. Our family calls it 'Dalmatian glitter'!*
>
> JACLYN HESLIP
> *Moen Lake Dalmatians*
>
> "

Most Dalmatians' grooming needs can be done at home. There are still a few things that we strongly recommend seeing an expert about in the early days to learn how to take care of your Dalmatian (all paw related), but for the most part, you should be able to take care of your dog yourself. You'll also appreciate the help since your Dalmatian is probably going to be incredibly rambunctious and difficult to calm down for paw care. With proper training, your Dalmatian can learn to endure grooming, realizing that it is dedicated time with you! It is also healthier for the dog if you do most of the grooming, as there are some issues that you are more likely to notice if you brush him daily (See Chapters 16 and 17.)

Here's a quick summary of the best tools to take care of your Dalmatian's coat:

- **Rubber brush**—and you can get a grooming glove to make it feel more like extra petting time instead of work
- **Shampoo** (Make sure you use dog shampoo, not human, and check Bark Space for the latest recommendations.)
- **Nail trimmers** and boar **bristle brush**
- **Toothbrush** and **dog toothpaste** (not human—it's toxic for dogs! Check the AKC for the latest recommendations for Dalmatians, as they tend to have dental problems.)

Coat Management

> **"**
>
> *One of our favorite things about Dalmatians is they don't have a strong dog smell. And they clean themselves, much like cats, so they require very little grooming.*
>
> RACHEL T.
> *The Spotted Dog Minnesota Dalmatians*
> **"**

Dalmatians are prolific shedders, so to reduce the amount of dog hair around your home, it is best to brush your dog daily. They have sensitive skin, so don't apply too much pressure when brushing. You can also remove some of the extra loose fur by using a blow dryer before putting your dog in the bath.

Always make sure to tire your dog before you start brushing. You'll know when you don't need to dedicate time to tiring your dog when he starts to slow down as a senior or shows an interest in just sitting and letting you pet and brush him.

Puppies

The difficulty when grooming a puppy is fairly universal because puppies are notorious for squirming! A daily brushing is the best way to bond with your dog and get him accustomed to grooming. Yes, it will be a bit challenging in the beginning because puppies don't sit still for prolonged periods of time; there will be a lot of wiggling and attempts to play. Trying to tell your puppy that the brush is not a toy clearly won't work, so be patient during each brushing session!

On the other hand, your pup will be so adorable that you probably won't mind a grooming session taking a bit longer than expected. Just make sure you let him know grooming is serious business, and playing comes after grooming. Otherwise, your Dalmatian is going to always try to play, which will make brushing time-consuming.

Try planning to brush your puppy after a vigorous exercise session. If you find your puppy has trouble sitting still, you can make brushing sessions shorter, but do it more than once a day until he gets used to the routine.

HELPFUL TIP

The Perfect Brush

Dalmatians have a short, wiry coat that requires minimal maintenance. The best brush for this type of fur is a rubber brush or grooming mitt, which helps remove loose fur and redistribute healthy oil throughout your Dalmatian's coat. A slicker brush is another great tool in your arsenal to remove loose fur and the unlikely tangle.

Adult Dogs

Brushing needs to be done at least once a week for adults, especially after a lot of outdoor activity. The grooming process stimulates the skin to release oils that make the fur shinier and more resistant to dirt. This is absolutely necessary for Dalmatians. If you regularly brush your dog, it can help reduce how often you have to bathe him.

Brushing your dog is about more than just removing excess fur and improving the coat's shine. You need to spend each grooming session looking for skin problems, lumps, flea or tick bites, and other problems when you brush your buddy. This will reveal any potential issues that you should monitor and follow up with a trip to the vet if symptoms become severe.

If you rescued an adult Dalmatian, it might take a little while to get the dog used to being brushed frequently. If your dog does not feel comfortable in the beginning when you brush his fur, work the routine into your schedule, just like training, so he will get accustomed to the task.

Senior Dogs

You can brush your senior dog more often if you would like, as the extra affection and time you give him will likely be welcome. The grooming process can be welcomed in older Dalmatians. After all, he's slowing

Photo Courtesy of
Deanne Angell

down, and just relaxing with you will be enjoyable for him (and the warmth of your hands will feel really good on his aging body). Grooming sessions are an appropriate time to check for problems while giving your older pup a nice massage to ease any pain. Look for any changes to the skin, such as bumps or fatty lumps. These may need to be mentioned to the vet during a regular visit.

Allergies

Dalmatians have sensitivity to allergens such as dust mites and pollen. Many Dals are sensitive to certain grasses, plants, and shampoos. Always have Benadryl handy. Your vet can prescribe soothing creams and lotions to help your Dal's skin and coat get better.

DEBBIE BENNETT
Westview Dalmatians

Many Dalmatians have skin allergies, so keep an eye out for hot spots, or if you notice your dog's coat is thinning, then you should look for the following allergic reactions:

- Wounds take longer to heal
- Weak immune system
- Aching joints
- Hair is falling out
- Ear infections
- Frequent scratching of the eyes

Regular brushing keeps you aware of the health of your Dalmatian's coat. This will help you identify when your big dear is suffering from allergies so that you can take him to the vet immediately.

Bath Time

> 66
>
> *Do not bathe your Dalmatian! Contrary to popular belief, they do not need weekly baths. Dals can have sensitive skin. If they are muddy after a decent hike, crate them for 30 minutes and the mud will drop right off their short coat! The crate will need cleaning, but that is easier and less time-consuming than bathing the dog. We only bathe before shows and if they have rolled in something gross. A rubber curry brush is all you need for helping to loosen and remove any excess hair.*
>
> MICHELLE POTTER
> *Symphony Dalmatians*
>
> 99

Baths are recommended roughly every six to eight weeks. If your Dalmatian gets muddy or really dirty, make sure to bathe him so that the dirt and mud don't get trapped in the fur and create worse problems. If you have medicinal shampoo, you will need to wash your dog twice, once with a hypo-allergenic shampoo, and a second time with the medicinal shampoo. Don't combine them. There's definitely a fine balance to bathing Dalmatians because they require bathing more often than a lot

Photo Courtesy of
Luis Martinez

of other dogs, but it is also very easy to over-bathe them, thinking that it will help keep them clean (when it will actually reduce their natural oils).

Make sure the water isn't too cold or too hot but comfortably warm, and always avoid getting your dog's head wet. How to wash your dog's face is covered in the next section.

12 STEPS FOR BATH TIME

1. Gather everything you will need before you start your dog's bath. At a minimum, you need the following:
   - shampoo and conditioners made specifically for dogs
   - cup for pouring water (if bathing in a tub)
   - towels
   - brushes for after the drying process
   - nonslip tub mat if you use a tub
   - buckets and a hose to rinse off if you bathe your dog outside

2. Take your Dalmatian out for a walk. This will tire your dog and make him a little hotter and less fearful—he might even appreciate the bath's cooling effect.

3. Run the water, making sure the temperature is lukewarm and not hot, especially if you have just finished a walk. If you are washing your Dalmatian in a bathtub, you only need enough water to cover your pup's stomach. Do not fully cover your dog's body.

4. Pick up your dog if you are using a bathtub, and talk to him in a strong, confident voice.

5. Place the dog in the tub, and use the cup to wash the dog. Don't use too much soap—it isn't necessary. You can fully soak the dog, starting at the neck and going to the rump. It is fine to get him wet and suds him up all at once, or you can do it a little at a time if your dog is very wiggly. Just make sure you don't get any water on his head.

6. Confidently talk to your Dalmatian while you are bathing him.

7. Make sure you don't pour water on your dog's head or in his eyes or ears. Use a wet hand and gently scrub. (Follow the steps in the next section for how to carefully wash your dog's face and ears.)

8. When you rinse, make sure to brush up against the fur so that there is no shampoo left.

9. Take your Dalmatian out of the water and towel him dry.

10. Make sure to give special attention to drying around the head and face.

11. Brush your dog when you are finished.

12. Give him a treat if he was particularly upset about the bath.

You can use these practices with other kinds of bathing, such as outside or at a public washing facility; modify the steps as necessary.

The first few times you bathe your dog, pay attention to the things that bother or scare your Dalmatian. If he is afraid of running water, make sure you don't have the water running when your dog is in the tub. If he moves around a lot when you start to apply the shampoo, it could indicate the smell is too strong. Modify the process as necessary in order to make it as comfortable for your dog as possible.

Keep a calm, loving tone as you wash your dog to make the process a little easier next time. Sure, your Dalmatian may whine, throw a tantrum, or wiggle excessively, but a calm reaction will teach your dog that bathing is a necessary part of being a member of the pack.

Cleaning Eyes and Ears

66

Grooming is important in order to keep bacteria away from your Dalmatian's ears, teeth, and paws. Depending on the climate, you have a higher risk of health problems based on the state. Georgia, for instance, is known for mold, bugs, and bacteria in the summer heat. I use Zymox on my adult dogs, and it always saves me a trip to the veterinarian. For the paws, an electric paw cleaner helps after they've gone hiking or swimming.

REBECCA BIERKO
Georgia Dalmatians

99

When bathing your dog, use a washcloth to wash his face and ears, and ALWAYS avoid getting water in his ears, which can lead to problems.

You will need to make weekly checks around your Dalmatian's eyes and ears to detect infections early. The following are signs of a problem:

- Frequent head shaking or tilting
- Regular scratching at ears

- Swollen or red ears
- A smell or discharge from the ears

If you notice any problems with your Dalmatian's ears, make an appointment with your vet. Never try to treat an infection on your own; hydrogen peroxide, cotton swabs, and other cleaning tools should never be used in a dog's ears. Your vet can show you how to clean your dog's ears correctly.

Dalmatians have a few genetic eye and ear conditions (See Chapter 17), so always take time to check your dog's eyes while you are grooming him.

Cataracts are a fairly common problem for all dogs as they age. If you see cloudy eyes, have your Dalmatian checked by your vet.

Trimming Nails

> 66
>
> *Dilute your shampoo to one part shampoo, three parts water. They have sensitive skin and many shampoos can be too harsh. Brush them out a couple of times a month and cut their toenails, please!*
>
> CAROL CHASE HEALY
> *Fiacre Dalmatians and Parson Russell Terriers*
> 99

If you have never cut a dog's nails before, do NOT start with a Dalmatian. Schedule an appointment with a professional groomer who has worked with large dogs before. There is a lot more work to do than just trimming the nails, and NO novice should ever attempt this grooming activity without a lot of guidance and help. A professional can show you what needs to be done to trim the nails. It is far harder to do with large dogs than with smaller ones.

Your professional can tell you what you need to know and let you know how often your dog needs his nails trimmed based on how quickly you help wear down the nails. If you and your Dalmatian spend a lot of time walking on sidewalks and concrete, it will slow the nail growth compared to regular jaunts in woods and dirt paths.

Oral Health

Dalmatians are prone to dental issues, and that means that you should never skip brushing your dog's teeth. Besides healthy food, there are two recommendations for taking care of your Dalmatian's teeth:

- Brush your Dalmatian's teeth at least twice a week.
- Give your Dalmatian dental chew treats.

Brushing Your Dog's Teeth

You have to learn to be patient and keep teeth cleaning from being an all-out fight with your dog. Brushing a dog's teeth is a little weird, and your Dalmatian may not be terribly happy with someone putting stuff in his mouth. However, once he is accustomed to it, the task will

Photo Courtesy of Tiffany Gromacki

likely only take a few minutes a day. Regular brushing keeps down plaque and tartar, making your pup's teeth healthier.

Always use a toothpaste that is made for dogs; human toothpaste can be toxic for your big friend. There are assorted flavors of dog toothpaste, which will make it easier when brushing your Dalmatian's teeth, and it could also be entertaining as he tries to eat the meat-flavored toothpaste!

The following are the steps for brushing your dog's teeth:

STEPS FOR BRUSHING YOUR DOG'S TEETH

1 Put a little toothpaste on your finger and hold it out to your dog.

2 Let your dog lick the toothpaste from your finger.

3 Praise your dog for trying something new.

4 Put a little toothpaste on your finger again, lift your dog's upper lip, and begin to rub in circles along your Dalmatian's gums. Your pup will likely make it difficult by constantly trying to lick your finger. Give your puppy praise when he doesn't lick the toothpaste or doesn't wiggle too much.

5 Try to move your finger in a circular motion. This will be very tricky, especially if you have a puppy with sharp baby teeth.

6 Try to keep the dog still without putting him in a vise. As your puppy gets bigger, he'll need to know how to sit for the cleaning process voluntarily.

7 Try to massage both the top and bottom gums. It is likely the first few times you won't be able to do much more than get your finger in your dog's mouth, and that's okay. Over time, your dog will learn to listen because general behavioral training will reinforce listening to your commands.

8 Stay positive. No, you probably won't be able to clean your dog's teeth properly for a while, and that is perfectly fine—as long as you keep working at it patiently and consistently.

Once your dog seems comfortable with having his teeth brushed with your finger, try the same steps with a canine toothbrush. (It could take a couple of weeks before you can graduate to this stage.)

Photo Courtesy of
Kayla Zornes

Dental Chews

One of the healthiest treats to give any dog is dental chews. While you will need to keep count of the treats as a part of your dog's daily caloric intake, they help with taking care of your dog's teeth. They aren't a replacement for regular brushing, but they are a good complement. Dogs tend to love these treats, and they help improve your dog's breath, so it is a win-win. Make sure to do your research to ensure that you are giving your dog the healthiest dental chews. You don't want to give your Dalmatian any treats that have questionable ingredients.

CHAPTER 16

General Health Issues: Allergies, Parasites, and Vaccinations

Since this is a dog that is probably going to love to be outside, you are going to want to make sure to monitor for allergies, look for parasites, and keep your dog vaccinated. All of these are going to be concerns for you and your Dalmatian. You will have some unique challenges with looking for parasites because of the black spots that will hide things like ticks. Dalmatians also tend to have allergies, which will cause them discomfort and itchiness.

For the most part, Dalmatian allergies appear on the skin, with rashes and hair loss being quite common, but sometimes they may scratch at their eyes. Adopting a daily brushing schedule will ensure that you not only notice rashes but will also be able to find any potential parasites infecting the exterior of your dog. If you notice your Dalmatian pawing at his eyes, this could also be a sign of allergies.

Environmental factors largely determine whether or not your dog gets parasites. For example, if you live near a wooded area, your dog is at a greater risk of having ticks than a dog that lives in the city. Fleas are a universal problem for all dogs because fleas can live in any grass, short or long. If you notice rashes or signs of skin irritation, it could be an allergic reaction or symptoms of a parasite. Talk to your vet about potential environmental risks and any skin conditions you notice when you groom your dog.

Photo Courtesy of
Carol Mallia

The Role of Your Veterinarian

Scheduled veterinary visits, routine vaccinations, and regular check-ups make for a healthy Dalmatian. If your dog seems sluggish or less excited than usual, it could be a sign there is something wrong with him. Fortunately, the breed's personality tends to make it easy to tell when your dog isn't feeling well. Annual visits to the vet will help catch any problems that might be slowly draining the energy or the health from your dog.

Regular check-ups also ensure that your Dalmatian is aging well. If your dog shows symptoms of a potential problem, an early diagnosis will address the problem. You and your vet can create a plan to manage any pain or problems that come with your dog's aging process. The vet may recommend adjustments to your schedule to accommodate your pup's aging body and diminishing abilities. This will ensure that the two of you can keep having fun together without hurting your dog.

Vets can provide treatment or preventive medication for parasites and other microscopic threats that your dog might encounter on a daily basis, whether playing outside or when he is exposed to dogs or other animals.

Photo Courtesy of Sara Radtke & Brian Fijal

Allergies

Allergies are a common problem for Dalmatians; if you see your dog scratching a lot, there are very good odds the problem is allergies. Dog allergies are usually a result of allergens (such as dust, mold, or pollen), which irritate the skin or nasal passages. Dogs often develop allergies when they are between one and five years old. Once they develop an allergy, canines never outgrow the problem.

The scientific name for environmental allergies is atopic dermatitis. However, it is difficult to know if the problem is environmental or if it is a food you are feeding your dog.

The following symptoms can be seen when either type of allergy is present:

- Itching/scratching, particularly around the face
- Hot spots
- Ear infections
- Skin infections
- Runny eyes and nose (not as common)

Since the symptoms are the same for food and environmental allergies, your vet will help determine the cause. If your dog has a food allergy, change the food that you give him. If he has an environmental allergy, he will need medication, just as humans do. There are several types of medications that can help your dog become less sensitive to allergens:

- **Antibacterial/Antifungal** – These treatments only address the problems that come with allergies; shampoos, pills, and creams usually do not directly treat the allergy itself.
- **Anti-inflammatories** – These are over-the-counter medications that are comparable to allergy medicine for people. Don't give your dog any medication without first consulting with the vet. You will need to monitor your dog to see if he has any adverse effects. If your dog is lethargic, has diarrhea, or shows signs of dehydration, consult with your vet immediately.
- **Immunotherapy** – This is a series of shots that can help reduce your dog's sensitivity to whatever he is allergic to. You can learn from your vet how to give your dog these shots at home. Scientists are also developing an oral version of this medication to make it easier to take care of your dog.
- **Topical** – This medication is usually a type of shampoo and conditioner that will remove any allergens from your dog's fur. Giving your dog a warm (not hot) bath can also help relieve itching.

To determine the best treatment for your situation, talk with your vet.

Inhalant and Environmental Allergies

Inhalant allergies are caused by things like dust, pollen, mold, and dog dander. Your dog might scratch at a particular hot spot, or he might paw at his eyes and ears. Some dogs have runny noses and sneeze prolifically, in addition to scratching.

HEALTH ALERT

Bronzing Skin

Dalmatian bronzing skin syndrome (DBS) is a skin condition that uniquely affects Dalmatians. This condi-tion, known as "Dal Crud," is character-ized by a darkening or bronzing stripe of discoloration from the Dalma-tian's head to tail. Hair loss and inflammation are also symptoms of this syndrome. DBS is thought to be hereditary and must be confirmed with a skin biopsy.

Contact Allergies

Contact allergies mean that your dog has touched something that triggers an allergic reaction. Substances like wool, chemicals in a flea treatment, and certain grasses can trigger irritation in a dog's skin, even causing discoloration. If left untreated, the allergic reaction can cause the affected area to emit a strong odor or cause fur loss.

Like food allergies, contact allergies are easy to treat because once you know what is irritating your dog's skin, you can remove the problem.

Fleas and Ticks

Make it a habit to check for ticks after every outing into the woods or near long grass or wild plants. Comb through your dog's fur and check his skin for signs of irritation and for any parasites. Since you will be brushing him a couple of times a week, you should be able to recognize when there's a change, such as a new bump.

Fleas are problematic because they're far more mobile than ticks. The best way to look for fleas is to make it a regular part of your brushing sessions. If you see black specks on the comb after brushing through your dog's fur, this could be a sign of fleas.

Instead of using a comb, you can also put your dog on a white towel and run your hand over his fur. Fleas and flea dirt are likely to fall onto the towel. Fleas often are seen on the stomach, so you may notice them when your pup wants a belly rub. You can also look for behavioral indicators, such as incessant scratching and licking. If fleas are a problem, you will need to use flea-preventative products on a regular basis once your puppy has reached the appropriate age.

Both fleas and ticks can carry parasites and illnesses that can be passed on to you and your family. Ticks carry Lyme disease, which can be debilitating or deadly if untreated. Lyme disease symptoms include headaches, fever, and fatigue. The bite itself often has a red circle around it.

Ticks will fall off your dog once they are full, so if you find a tick on your dog, it will either be looking for a place to latch onto your dog, or it will be feeding. Use the following steps to remove the tick if it has latched onto your dog.

1. Apply rubbing alcohol to the area where the tick is located.
2. Use tweezers to pull the tick off your dog. Do not use your fingers—infections are transmitted through blood, and you don't want the tick to latch onto you.
3. Place the tick in a bag and make sure it is secure so that it does not fall out. The vet can assess the type of tick for diagnostic purposes since different types of ticks carry different diseases.

Photo Courtesy of Monika Talanga

4. Examine the spot where the tick was to make sure it is fully removed. Sometimes the head will remain under the dog's skin, so make sure all of the tick has been removed.
5. Set up a meeting with the vet to have your dog checked.

The FDA has issued a warning about some store-bought treatments for fleas and ticks. Treatments can be applied monthly, or you can purchase a collar for constant protection. Either way, make sure the treatment does not contain isoxazoline, which can have a negative effect on some pets. (This chemical is found in Bravecto, Nexgard, Credelio, and Simparica.)

Most ingredients in these treatments are safe if the proper dose is used. However, if you use a product that is meant for a larger dog, the effects can be toxic to your smaller dog or not as effective if you use a dosage meant for a smaller dog on your large dog. Consult your vet for recommended treatments and administer the appropriate dose of flea and tick repellant for your dog's size and needs. When you start applying the treatment, watch your dog for the following issues:

- Diarrhea/vomiting
- Trembling
- Lethargy
- Seizures

Take your dog to the vet if you notice any of these issues.

Never use any cat product on a dog and vice versa. If your dog is sick, pregnant, or nursing, you may need to look for an alternative preventative treatment. If you have a cat or young children, you should choose one of the other preventative options for keeping fleas and ticks away. This is because flea collars contain an ingredient that is lethal to felines and which might be carcinogenic to humans.

The packaging on flea treatments will advise you when to begin treating your dog based on his current age and size. Different brands have different recommendations, and you don't want to start treating your puppy too early. There are also important steps to applying the treatment. Make sure you understand all of the steps before purchasing the flea treatment.

If you want to use natural products instead of chemicals, research the alternatives and decide what works best for your Dalmatian. Verify that any natural products work before you buy them, and make sure you consult with your vet. Establish a regular monthly schedule and add it to your calendar so that you remember to consistently treat your dog for fleas and ticks.

Parasitic Worms

Although worms are a less common problem in dogs than fleas and ticks, they can be far more dangerous. The following lists the types of worms that you should be aware of:

- Heartworms
- Hookworms

Photo Courtesy of
@Charleymae.DogPhotography

- Roundworms
- Tapeworms
- Whipworms

Unfortunately, there isn't an easy-to-recognize set of symptoms to help identify when your dog has worms. However, you can keep an eye out for the following symptoms, and if your dog shows any of these warning signs, schedule a visit to the vet:

- Your Dalmatian is unexpectedly lethargic for a few days.
- Patches of fur begin to fall out (this will be noticeable if you brush your Dalmatian regularly), or you notice patchy spaces in your dog's coat.
- Your dog's stomach becomes distended (expands) and looks like a potbelly.
- Your Dalmatian begins coughing or vomiting, has diarrhea, or has a loss of appetite.

If you aren't sure about any symptom, it's always best to get your dog to the vet as soon as possible.

Heartworms

Heartworms are a significant threat to your dog's health and can be deadly as they can both slow and stop blood flow. As such, you should consistently treat your dog with heartworm protection.

Fortunately, there are medications that prevent your dog from developing heartworms. To prevent this deadly problem, you can give your dog a chewable medication, use a topical medicine, or request shots.

The heartworm parasite is carried by mosquitoes, and it is a condition that is costly and time-consuming to treat. The following are the steps involved in treating your dog for heartworms:

- The vet will draw blood for testing, which can cost as much as $1,000.
- Treatment will begin with some initial medications, including antibiotics and anti-inflammatory drugs.
- Following a month of the initial medication, your vet will give your dog three shots over the course of two months.

From the time of diagnosis until the confirmation your dog is free of heartworms, you will need to be extremely cautious when you exercise him because the worms are in his heart, and that inhibits blood flow. This means raising your dog's heart rate too much could kill him. Your vet will tell you how best to exercise your canine during this time. Considering your Dalmatian may want to be energetic, this could be a very rough time for both you and your dog.

Treatment will continue after the shots are complete. After approximately six months, your vet will conduct another blood test to ensure the worms are gone.

Photo Courtesy of Amy Burdis

Once your dog is cleared of the parasites, you will need to begin medicating him against heartworms in the future. There will be lasting damage to your dog's heart, so you will need to ensure that he does not overexercise.

Intestinal Worms: Hookworms, Roundworms, Tapeworms, and Whipworms

All four of these worms thrive in your dog's intestinal tract, and they get there when he eats something contaminated. The following are the most common ways dogs ingest worms:

- Feces
- Small hosts, such as fleas, cockroaches, earthworms, and rodents
- Soil, including licking it from their fur and paws
- Contaminated water

- Mother's milk (If the mother dog has worms, she can pass them on to young puppies when they nurse.)

The following are the most common symptoms and problems caused by intestinal parasites:

- Anemia
- Blood loss
- Coughing
- Dehydration
- Diarrhea
- Large intestine inflammation
- Weight loss
- A pot-bellied appearance

If a dog lies in soil with **hookworm larvae**, the parasites can burrow through the canine's skin. Your vet will conduct a diagnostic test to determine if your dog has this parasite, and if he does, the vet will prescribe a dewormer. If your dog is infested with hookworms, you should visit a doctor yourself because humans can get hookworms too. Being treated at the same time as your Dalmatian will help stop the vicious cycle of continually trading off which of you has hookworms.

Photo Courtesy of Cassandra Vela

Roundworms are quite common, and at some point in their lives, most dogs have to be treated for them. The parasites primarily eat the digested food in your dog's stomach, getting the nutrients he needs. It is possible for larvae to remain in your dog's stomach even after all the adult worms have been eradicated. If your Dalmatian is pregnant, her puppies should be checked periodically to make sure the inactive larvae are not passed on to them. The mother will also need to go through the same testing to make sure the worms don't make her sick.

Photo Courtesy of Justin Hocking

Tapeworms are usually eaten when they are eggs and are carried by fleas or in the feces of other animals that also have tapeworms. The eggs develop in the canine's small intestine until they reach the adult stage. Over time, parts of the tapeworm will break off and can be seen in your dog's waste. If this happens, you should be very thorough when cleaning up any waste so other animals will not also contract tapeworms. While tapeworms are not usually fatal, they can cause weight loss and give your dog a potbelly. (The size of your dog's stomach depends on how big the worms grow in his intestines.)

Your vet can test your dog for tapeworms and can prescribe medication to take care of the problem. The medication might include chewable tablets, regular tablets, or a powder that can be sprinkled on your dog's food. There is a minimal risk of humans catching tapeworms, but children are at the greatest risk. Be sure children wash their hands carefully when playing in areas used by your dog. It is also possible to contract tapeworms if a person swallows a flea, which is feasible if your dog and home have a serious infestation.

Whipworms grow in the large intestine, and when in large numbers, they can be fatal. Their name is indicative of the appearance of their tails, which are thinner than their upper section. Like the other worms, you will need to have your dog tested to determine if he has acquired whipworms.

Staying current with flea treatments, properly disposing of your pet's waste, and making sure your Dalmatian does not eat trash or animal waste will help prevent him from getting these parasites.

Medication to prevent these four parasites can often be included in your dog's heartworm medication. Be sure to speak with your vet regarding the different options.

Vaccinating Your Dalmatian

Vaccination schedules are routine for most dog breeds, including Dalmatians. Make sure to add this information to your calendar, and until your puppy has completed his vaccinations, he should avoid contact with other dogs.

The following list can help you schedule your Dalmatian's vaccinations:

Timeline	Shot
6 to 8 weeks	Bordetella • Leptospira • DHPP – First shot Lyme • Influenza Virus-H3N8 • Influenza Virus-H3N2
10 to 12 weeks	Leptospira • DHPP – Second Rabies shot Lyme • Influenza Virus-H3N8 • Influenza Virus-H3N2
14 to 16 weeks	DHPP – Third shot
Annually	Leptospira • Bordetella • Rabies Lyme • Influenza Virus-H3N8 • Influenza Virus-H3N2
Every 3 years	DHPP Booster • Rabies (if opting for a longer-duration vaccination)

These shots protect your dog against a range of ailments. Keep in mind these shots should be a part of your dog's annual vet visit so you can continue to keep your pup safe!

Holistic Alternatives

Wanting to prevent exposure to chemical treatments for your dog makes sense, and there are many good reasons why people are moving to more holistic methods. However, if you decide to go with holistic medication, talk with your vet first about reputable options. You can also seek out Dalmatian experts for recommendations before you start trying any holistic methods of care.

It is possible something like massage therapy can help your dog, especially as he ages. Even chiropractic therapy is available for dogs, but you will need to be sure to find a reputable chiropractor for your pup so that the treatment doesn't do more harm than good. Follow recommendations on reputable, holistic Dalmatian websites to provide the best, safest care for your dog.

CHAPTER 17

Genetic Health Concerns Common to Dalmatians

Although Dalmatians were healthy over most of their history, the release of a movie about them created a big demand for Dalmatian puppies. Because of this, the breed suffered, with breeders paying more attention to the money they could make over the health of the puppies. This led to a rise in the number of issues associated with Dalmatians. Many of those issues are not life-threatening, but they will affect your dog's quality of life.

Photo Courtesy of Kelly Norton

Proper care, including watching your dog's weight can help keep your dog from having a lot of health issues. Chapter 15 covered how to keep your dog healthy with a good diet, and 16 covered how to protect your dog from outside risks. This chapter focuses on genetic issues, their symptoms, and how the ailments are treated. It also covers the kinds of ailments that come with age, something that you will likely start to notice by the time your Dalmatian is eight years old.

Common Dalmatians Health Issues

You want to make sure that you catch health issues early to improve your dog's quality of life. Take the time to monitor your dog for those potential health problems.

Deafness

"

Dalmatians, like many other white dogs, are prone to deafness. A BAER (brainstem auditory evoked response) hearing test is recommended for every Dalmatian puppy at about six to eight weeks old. A BAER hearing test will let potential owners know if a puppy is deaf in one ear or both ears. A puppy who is deaf in one ear will probably live a normal life but should never be bred to have puppies. A puppy that is completely deaf will have unique challenges and require a household that is ready to take on those challenges. Deaf Dalmatians can still make great pets, but they are not for everyone.

RACHEL T.
The Spotted Dog Minnesota Dalmatians

"

Dalmatians are more prone to deafness than almost any other breed. It is estimated that between 15 and 30% of Dalmatians have minor to complete deafness. It is a genetic condition that is tied to the same thing that causes their gorgeous coat. The problem is related to the reduced production of melanin cells in the breed's ears. Melanin is required for normal hearing.

Dogs don't need to have fantastic hearing to live happy lives, but they do require that you adjust how you work with them. Fortunately, this is a smart breed, and Dalmatians can learn sign language. They are also quite adept at learning how to work around their hearing loss.

Never take them off leash outside of your fenced-in yard because they will not be able to hear you to stop or respond when you call them.

Bladder Stones and Urinary Problems

> 66
>
> *Dalmatians are genetically predisposed to form urate stones when there are too many purines in their food. They must have an easily digestible, low-protein diet. They must have clean, fresh water every day. Encourage your dog to drink lots of water every day. Don't let him go more than four hours without peeing. When your dog can't pee (or it just dribbles out) take him to the vet immediately. It is a life-threatening situation. There are low-uric-acid Dalmatians available (Dals that don't form urate stones) but, again, do your research. There are bad breeders at all levels.*
>
> CAROL CHASE HEALY
> *Fiacre Dalmatians and Parson Russell Terriers*
>
> 99

Dalmatians seem more prone to getting uric acid stones, which can become life threatening because the stones can block the urinary tract. One of the most common symptoms is that your dog will have trouble urinating, which means little to no urine will come out, even after hours of the dog being inside. It could also cause your dog to have trouble controlling where he urinates, so it may cause your dog to have accidents.

This problem is pretty easily treated through medication for minor cases. More severe cases may require surgery. Diet and medication may also prevent your dog from developing the problem. You can have your dog tested to see if he is prone to the problem.

Skin Ailments

> **"**
>
> *Dalmatians can have allergies that usually manifest as itching. Your veterinarian can help decide if medication or food changes are necessary. Bladder stones can also be a problem. Regular veterinary care and observing your dog's urination will help detect changes early.*
>
> SARAH GROTE, DVM
> *Willing Hearts Dalmatian Rescue*
>
> **"**

The uniqueness of the Dalmatian's coat comes with several skin issues.

Dalmatian Bronzing Syndrome

Also called Dal Crud, this problem appears as a strip of either pink or bronze color that goes from the dog's head to the tail. It can also cause hair loss, and in some cases, the hair follicles may become inflamed. It is thought to be genetic. One of discoloration and follicle issues, it could also make the dog more susceptible to other skin problems.

If you notice your dog having the symptoms of the disease, your vet can do a skin biopsy to determine if this is the root cause. There is no treatment, but it can be managed to keep it from causing problems. Often it is treated with something as simple as fish oil supplements or a specially prescribed shampoo.

Atopy

Atopy is simply a sensitivity to allergens, something that most of us experience. The difference is that dogs show their allergies differently, with symptoms showing up on their skin. Anything can trigger a reaction, such as dust mites and pollen. Dogs who have this condition may itch more. Fortunately, it is easy to deal with this problem by reducing exposure to the cause of the issue and using shampoos and other cleaning agents for your dog's coat that will help protect him.

Eye Issues

Those gorgeous eyes are also prone to problems. Fortunately, they generally don't cause significant complications, especially if you catch them early and treat them.

HEALTH ALERT
Copper Storage Disease

Copper storage disease (CSD) is a hereditary condition that affects Dalmatians, resulting in the accumula-tion of copper in the liver cells. This disorder is caused by a mutation in a gene responsible for regulating copper metabolism. As Dalmatians lack certain liver enzymes, they are unable to efficiently process and excrete copper, leading to its buildup over time. CSD can cause liver damage and dysfunction, leading to symptoms such as jaundice, weight loss, and increased thirst. Early detection through liver function tests and liver biopsies is crucial for managing CSD. Treatment involves a low-copper diet, medications, and supportive care to maintain liver health in affected Dalmatians.

Glaucoma

A painful eye ailment, glaucoma can result in blindness if it isn't treated early. If you notice your Dalmatian's eyes watering a lot, the cornea turning blue, or your dog squinting often, get him to the vet. These are signs that your dog is in pain, which can be difficult to notice because you get accustomed to the behavior.

You can also have your vet do an annual glaucoma screening.

Entropion

Entropion is when the dog's eyelids roll inward, damaging the cornea as the eyelashes scratch it. The corrective surgery that fixes this problem can cause another eye disorder, ectropion. This is when the lower eyelid droops down so that you can see the soft pink tissue under the eye. While ectropion is not a serious problem—Basset Hounds live with it as a natural part of their facial structure—it does increase the likelihood of eye infections.

Iris Sphincter Dysplasia

This medical issue is more commonly found in Dalmatians with liver spots but may be found in other Dalmatians at a lower rate. It causes the dog's pupils to look like they are perpetually dilated, caused by the muscles around the eyes not working properly. If your dog has this problem, they will be more sensitive to light. It may also make your dog more susceptible to other eye problems.

Epilepsy

Epilepsy is a neurological disorder that causes seizures, and Dalmatians are a breed that is prone to having it. If your dog starts to have seizures, you need to get him to a vet. Your dog can live a happy, healthy life with early intervention. When left untreated, epilepsy can cause brain damage, and in severe cases, it can cause death.

Photo Courtesy of Nikki Brackley

Hypothyroidism

This is a problem that is also found in humans (and many other dog breeds). Hypothyroidism is a result of the body not making enough thyroid hormone. It often begins to show in a Dalmatian by age six, and symptoms include weight gain, lack of energy, and skin problems (such as dry or itchy skin).

Photo Courtesy of Sasha Bubenik

A blood test is done to find out if a Dalmatian has hypothyroidism. Some vets will conduct the test annually as a preventative measure. If your dog has hypothyroidism, your vet will likely prescribe an oral medication.

Hip Dysplasia

Hip dysplasia is a common ailment for medium- and larger-sized dogs. A dog's diet (Chapter 14) as a puppy can help minimize the problem as an adult. Both types of dysplasia are a result of the dog's hip and leg sockets being malformed, and that often leads to arthritis because the improper fit damages cartilage. The condition is possible to detect by X-ray when a dog becomes an adult.

This is a problem that your Dalmatian may try to hide because he won't want to slow down. Your adult dog will walk a little more stiffly or may pant even when it's not hot. It usually becomes more obvious as a dog nears his golden years; similar to the way older people tend to change their gait to accommodate pain, your dog may do the same thing. Getting up may be a little more difficult in the beginning and will likely get worse as he ages.

233

While surgery is an option in severe cases, most dogs can benefit from less invasive treatment:

Photo Courtesy of Amy Jackson

- Anti-inflammatory medications – Talk to your vet (Dogs should not have large doses of anti-inflammatory drugs on a daily basis since aspirin and anti-inflammatories can damage his kidneys.)
- Lower the amount of high-impact exercise your dog gets, especially on wood floors, tile, concrete, or other hard surfaces. Given how much your dog probably loves to swim, you can move more to a swimming exercise regimen to keep him active without the jarring motions of walking and jogging on hard surfaces.
- Joint fluid modifiers
- Physical therapy
- Weight loss (for dogs who are overweight or obese)

Copper-Associated Liver Disease

When a dog has too much copper accumulated in his liver, it can cause him to appear jaundiced. However, not all dogs actually show any symptoms, which could be a problem if they have too much copper in their system.

Dogs that have been diagnosed should be treated with supplements and medications.

Dilated Cardiomyopathy

This is a life-threatening condition where the dog's heart is enlarged, often causing it to have thinner walls. It also weakens the heart, which

Photo Courtesy of
Gitana Dainauskas

can cause some significant issues. There are a number of symptoms associated with this ailment, including the following:

- Heavy breathing when resting or sleeping
- Trouble breathing
- Restless sleep
- Coughing
- Gagging
- Reduced levels of energy
- Fainting
- Decreased appetite
- Weight loss
- Distended belly
- Depressed attitude or quiet and not interactive

There are a number of tests for the disease, including blood testing and EKG.

Once a dog is diagnosed with the condition, treatment should begin. There are a number of medications that can help to stabilize the problem and then to treat it over time. The condition does require aggressive treatment, and there is no guarantee that the medications will extend the life of the sufferer. There is no cure for the condition.

Common Owner Mistakes

In addition to genetic problems, there are things you can do that could unintentionally damage your dog's health; these mistakes are related to diet and exercise levels. In the puppy stage, it is a

Photo Courtesy of Ashleigh Vogl

HEALTH ALERT
Heart Disease

Dalmatians can be particularly susceptible to a heart condition called dilated cardiomyopathy (DCM). This condition manifests as an enlarged heart that can no longer pump blood effectively. Advanced signs of this condition include weakness, labored coughing, and collapse. Annual screenings can detect this condition early and improve your dog's prognosis with medication and dietary intervention.

difficult balance to strike as your puppy is curious and enthusiastic. Even when he is a fully grown dog, you have to make sure you are minimizing how much stress is placed on your Dalmatian's body. Weight management is one important way of keeping your dog healthy. You need to balance your dog's diet with his level of activity to prevent exacerbation of hip and elbow dysplasia.

Failing to notice early signs of potential issues can be detrimental or even fatal to your Dalmatian. Any changes in your Dalmatian's behavior are likely a sign of something that should be checked by your vet.

Prevention and Monitoring

> *Dalmatians have a genetic predisposition to forming urate urinary crystals and stones. Feeding an appropriate diet and ensuring proper hydration will minimize any risks. Copper storage disease has been found in most, if not all, lines if you look far enough back. To screen for any early signs of copper storage disease, Dalmatians should have blood work done at 12, 18, and 24 months, then annually.*
>
> HEATHER PARSONS
> *Bedlam Acres Dalmatians*

Checking your Dalmatian's weight is important and should be done at least once a quarter or twice a year. You and your vet should keep an eye on your dog's weight, as being overweight puts a strain on your dog's back, legs, joints, and muscles.

CHAPTER 18

The Aging Dalmatian

With a life span between 11 and 13 years, this is a dog that can give you many years of memories, but eventually, your Dalmatian will start to slow down. You play a large role in how long your Dalmatian lives because you are the one who controls how much he exercises, how nutritious his meals are, and how often he makes regular visits to the vet.

By the time Dalmatians are eight years old, they are considered senior dogs, so you need to start paying attention to how they react to all of their regular activities. It is highly unlikely that your Dalmatian will

Photo Courtesy of
Sammy Biggs

want to acknowledge that he's slowing down—no high-energy dog can easily accept this fact. This is why it is up to you to adjust his activities to meet any decline in health and abilities. As long as you continue to give him plenty of love and attention, your Dalmatian will be happy enough without two or more hours of activity a day. Just don't let the exercise completely drop off because your dog will still be fairly active.

Regular vet visits, age-appropriate food, and lots of love are the things that your older dog needs. Since this has probably been a pretty mellow dog for at least a few years now, you may already have a pretty good schedule set up. It may just be a matter of monitoring how much activity you guys enjoy. Watch your dog the next morning to make sure he isn't stiff after spending a day out hiking or doing another activity.

There is a reason these are called the golden years—you can really enjoy them with your dog. You don't have to worry as much about him tearing things up out of boredom or getting overexcited on walks anymore. You can enjoy lazy evenings and peaceful weekends with some less strenuous exercise to break up the day. It's easy to make the senior years enjoyable for your Dalmatian and yourself by making the necessary adjustments.

Senior Care Challenges

> *As with any aging dog, be sure to keep your Dalmatian exercised, groomed, and happy. Clean his teeth, cut his toenails, and brush him as you would a younger dog. At age seven, he should have a senior blood panel done each year, just so you know if any problems are cropping up. Senior love to do everything a younger Dal loves, but just remember their age and don't overdo.*
>
> CAROL CHASE HEALY
> *Fiacre Dalmatians and Parson Russell Terriers*

Photo Courtesy of
Zachary Boso

In most cases, caring for an older dog is simpler than taking care of a younger dog, and Dalmatians are no exception.

Accommodations you should make for your senior Dalmatian include:

- Set water bowls out in a couple of different places so that your dog can easily reach them as needed. If your Dalmatian shows signs of having trouble drinking or eating, place slightly raised water dishes around the home.
- Cover hard floor surfaces (such as tile, hardwood, and vinyl). Use nonslip carpets or rugs.
- Add cushions and softer bedding for your Dalmatian. This will both make the surface more comfortable and help him stay warmer. There are bed warmers for dogs if your Dalmatian has achy joints or muscles. Of course, you also need to make sure he isn't too warm, so this can be a fine balancing act.

- To improve his circulation, increase how often you brush your Dalmatian.
- Stay inside in extreme heat and cold. Your Dalmatian is hardy, but an old canine cannot handle extreme changes as well as he once did.
- Use stairs or ramps for your Dalmatian wherever possible so that the old pup doesn't have to try to jump.
- Avoid moving your furniture around, particularly if your Dalmatian shows signs of having trouble with his sight or has dementia. A familiar home is more comforting and less stressful as your pet ages. If your Dalmatian isn't able to see as clearly as he once did, keeping the home familiar will make it easier for him to move around without getting hurt.
- Consider setting up an area where your dog can stay without having to go up and down any stairs too often.
- Create a space where your Dalmatian can relax with fewer distractions and noises. Don't make your old friend feel isolated, but do give him a place to get away from everyone if he needs to be alone.
- Be prepared to let your dog out more often for restroom breaks.

Common Physical Disorders Related to Aging

Chapters 4 and 16 cover illnesses that are common or likely with a Dalmatian, but old age tends to bring a slew of ailments that aren't particular to any one breed. Here are the things you will need to watch for (as well as talk to your vet about).

- Diabetes is probably the greatest concern for a breed that loves to eat as much as your Dalmatian does. Although diabetes is usually thought of as a genetic condition, any Dalmatian can become diabetic if not fed and exercised properly.
- Arthritis is probably the most common ailment in any dog breed, and the Dalmatian is no exception. If your dog is showing signs of stiffness and pain after normal activities, talk with your vet about safe ways to help minimize the discomfort.

Photo Courtesy of
Charlene Yablonsky

- Gum disease is a common issue in older dogs as well, and you should be just as vigilant about toothbrushing when your dog gets older as at any other age. A regular check of your Dalmatian's teeth and gums can help ensure this does not become a problem.
- Loss of eyesight or blindness is relatively common in older dogs, just as it is in humans. Have your dog's vision checked at least once a year and more often if it is obvious that his eyesight is failing.

- Kidney disease is a common problem in older dogs and one that you should monitor the older your Dalmatian gets. If your canine is drinking more often and having accidents regularly, get your Dalmatian to the vet as soon as possible.

Steps and Ramps

You shouldn't pick your large Dalmatian up to carry him upstairs or put him in the car. Steps and ramps are the best way to safely ensure your Dalmatian can maintain some level of self-sufficiency as he ages. Also, using steps and ramps provides a bit of extra exercise.

If your Dalmatian has trouble seeing, you will need to make sure that you assist your dog up into cars or other inclines so that he doesn't get hurt. This can be difficult because your dog likely won't want to be less agile than he was in earlier years, so be supportive and give your dog a lot of praise so he knows that he's doing very well. Not only will your dog feel better about the lost abilities, but it will also be a great reminder that he's still a loved dog.

Adjusting the Exercise Routine

> 66
>
> *Dalmatians, like any dogs, are going to lose some agility, muscle mass, and motivation as they age. A Dalmatian will always want to run, play, and please its owner well into its advanced age—maybe just not as frequently. My advice is to love and care for your Dalmatian as hard and as long as you can. This is the time to return the love and loyalty he's shown you his entire life.*
>
> JACLYN HESLIP
> *Moen Lake Dalmatians*
>
> 99

Photo Courtesy of Kelsey Lewis

This one may be tough because your Dalmatian is going to want to keep joining you for the same activities, so leaving your dog behind for a long jog is going to be rough on your pup. You can break up his exercise into several trips out so that he has some time to recover between bouts, but it will help him to feel like he isn't missing out on too much. You will need to shorten trips, including walks, especially as he reaches over 10 years old.

Since your dog's brain isn't likely to slow down, you can change from high-energy activities to more low-key training and swimming in shallower waters. This can include doing more treasure hunting and other sniffing games since those are low impact; just make sure you don't go overboard on the treats since Dalmatians are less active in the later years.

Vet Visits

As your Dalmatian ages, you are going to notice the slowdown, and the pains in your Dalmatian's body are going to be obvious, just like they are in an older person. You need to make sure that you have regular visits with your vet to ensure you aren't doing anything that could potentially harm your Dalmatian. If your dog has a debilitating ailment or condition, you may want to discuss options for ensuring a better quality of life, such as wheels if your Dalmatian's legs begin to have serious issues.

The Importance of Regular Vet Visits

Just as humans go to visit the doctor more often as they age, you'll need to take your dog to see your vet with greater frequency. The vet can make sure that your Dalmatian is staying active without overdoing it and that there is no unnecessary stress on your older dog. If your canine has sustained an injury and hidden it from you, your vet is more likely to detect it.

Your vet can also make recommendations about activities and changes to your schedule based on your Dalmatian's physical abilities and any changes in personality. For example, if your Dalmatian is panting more now, it could be a sign of pain from stiffness. This could be difficult to distinguish given how much Dalmatians pant as a rule, but if you see other signs of pain, schedule a visit with the vet. Your vet can help you determine the best way to keep your Dalmatian happy and active during the later years.

What to Expect at Vet Visits

- Your vet is going to talk about your dog's history, even if you have visited every year. This talk is necessary to see how things have gone or if any possible problems have started to show or have gotten worse.
- While you chat, your vet will probably conduct a complete physical examination to assess your dog's health.
- Depending on how old your dog is and the kind of health he is in, your vet may want to run different tests. The following are some of the most common tests for older dogs.
  - Arthropod-borne disease testing, which involves drawing blood and testing it for viral infections
  - Chemistry screening for kidney, liver, and sugar evaluation
  - Complete blood count
  - Fecal flotation, which involves mixing your dog's poop with a special liquid to test for worms and other parasites
  - Heartworm testing
  - Urinalysis, which tests your dog's urine to check the health of your dog's kidneys and urinary system
- The same routine wellness check that the vet has been conducting on your dog all his life
- Any breed-specific tests for your aging Dalmatian

Changes to Watch For

Keep an eye out for different signs that your dog is slowing down. This will help you to know when to adjust the setup around your home and to reduce how much your old pup is exercising.

Appetite and Nutritional Requirements

> **"**
>
> *In my experience, most Dalmatians do not show their age until they are near the end of their life span. As they age, I like to give my dogs a good-quality vitamin with supplements like glucosamine and chondroitin to help support their joints.*
>
> EMILY HUF
> *Dream Chaser Dalmatians*
> **"**

With less exercise, your dog doesn't need as many calories, which means you need to adjust your pup's diet. If you opt to feed your Dalmatian commercial dog food, make sure you change to a senior food.

If you make your Dalmatian's food, talk to your vet and take the time to research how best to reduce calories without sacrificing taste. Your canine is going to need less fat in his food, so you may need to find something healthier that still has a lot of taste to supplement the types of foods you gave your Dalmatian as a puppy or active adult dog.

Exercise

Since Dalmatians are so gregarious, they are going to be just as happy with extra attention from you as they were with exercise when they were younger. If you make fewer demands, decrease the number of walks, or in any way change the routine, your Dalmatian will quickly adapt to the new program. You will need to make those changes based on your dog's ability, so it's up to you to adjust the schedule and keep your Dalmatian happily active. Shorter, more frequent walks should take care of your Dalmatian's exercise needs, as well as help to break up your day a little more.

Your dog will enjoy napping as much as walking, especially if he gets to cuddle with you. Sleeping beside you while you watch television or as you nap is pretty much all it takes to make your older Dalmatian content, but he still needs to exercise.

The way your Dalmatian slows down will probably be the hardest part of watching him age. You may notice that your Dalmatian spends more time sniffing during walks, which could be a sign that your dog is tiring. It could also be his way of acknowledging that long steady walks are a thing of the past, and so he is stopping to enjoy the little things more. Stopping to smell things may now give him the excitement that he used to get by walking farther.

While you should be watching for your dog to tire, he may also let you know. If he is walking slower, looking up at you, and flopping down, that could be his way of letting you know it's time to return home. If your canine can't manage long walks, make the walks shorter and more numerous and spend more time romping around your yard or home with your buddy.

Aging and the Senses

Just like people, dogs' senses weaken as they get older, and larger dogs' senses tend to deteriorate faster than smaller dogs. They won't hear things as well as they used to, they won't see things as clearly, and their sense of smell will weaken.

The following are some signs that your dog is losing at least one of his senses.

- It becomes easy to surprise or startle your dog. You need to be careful because this can make your Dalmatian aggressive, a scary prospect even in old age. Do NOT sneak up on your old dog, as this can be bad for both of you, and he deserves better than to be scared.
- Your dog may seem to ignore you because he is less responsive when you issue a command. If you have not had a problem before, your dog isn't being stubborn; he is likely losing his hearing.
- Cloudy eyes may be a sign of loss of sight, though it does not mean that your dog is blind.

If your dog seems to be "behaving badly," it is a sign that he is aging, not that he doesn't care or wants to rebel. Do not punish your older dog.

Adjust your schedule to meet your dog's changing abilities. Adjust water bowl height, refrain from rearranging rooms, and pet your dog more often. He is probably nervous about losing his abilities, so it is up to you to comfort him.

*Photo Courtesy of
Alan Hitchen*

Keeping Your Senior Dog Mentally Active

Just because your Dalmatian can't walk as far doesn't mean that his brain isn't just as focused and capable. As he slows down physically, focus more on activities that are mentally stimulating. As long as your Dalmatian has all of the basics down, you can teach him all kinds of low-impact tricks. At this point, training could be easier because your Dalmatian has learned to focus better, and he'll be happy to have something he can still do with you.

New toys are another great way to help keep your dog's mind active. Be careful that the toys aren't too rough on your dog's older jaw and teeth. Tug-of-war may be a game of the past (you don't want to hurt old teeth), but other games, such as hide-and-seek, will still be very much appreciated. Whether you hide toys or yourself, this can be a game that keeps your Dalmatian guessing. There are also food balls, puzzles, and other games that focus on cognitive abilities.

Some senior dogs suffer from cognitive dysfunction (CCD) syndrome, a type of dementia. It is estimated that 85% of all cases of dementia in dogs go undiagnosed because of the difficulty in pinpointing the problem. It manifests more as a problem of temperament.

If your dog begins to act differently, you should take him to the vet to see if he has CCD. While there really isn't any treatment for it, your vet can recommend things you can do to help your dog. Things like rearranging the rooms of your home are strongly discouraged, as familiarity with his surroundings will help your dog feel more comfortable and will reduce stress as he loses his cognitive abilities. Mental stimulation will help to fight CCD,

FUN FACT
The Oldest Dalmatian

Dalmatians enjoy a life span of about 10 to 14 years and are a generally healthy breed. The oldest documented Dalmatian was named Scootie and lived one month short of 21 years. Despite his longer-than-average life, Scootie was the runt of his litter, was diagnosed with cancer at 10 years old, and lived with a heart murmur. During the last two years of Scootie's life, he lost the ability to walk and suffered from poor eyesight. On March 9, 2018, he passed away.

but you should plan to keep your dog mentally stimulated regardless of whether or not he exhibits symptoms of dementia.

Advantages to the Senior Years

The last years of your Dalmatian's life can be just as enjoyable (if not more so) than the earlier stages since your dog will have mellowed. All of those high-energy activities will give way to cuddles and relaxation. Having your pup just enjoy your company can be incredibly nice (Just remember to keep up his activity levels instead of getting too complacent with your Dalmatian's newfound love of resting and relaxing.)

Your Dalmatian will continue to be a loving companion, interacting with you at every opportunity—that does not change with age. But your canine's limitations should dictate interactions and activities. If you are busy, make sure you schedule time with your Dalmatian to do things that are within those limitations. It is just as easy to make an older Dalmatian happy as it is with a young one, and it is easier on you since relaxing is more essential to your old friend.

Preparing to Say Goodbye

66

Love your Dalmatian till his last breath and dedicate your time to his health. It is harder for the dog as it develops health problems such as arthritis, blindness, and other health issues such as cancer. I like to recommend chiropractic care, animal nutritionists, and pet insurance. We all want what is best for our pets.

REBECCA BIERKO
Georgia Dalmatians

99

This is something that all dog parents (well, pet parents, really) don't want to think about, but as you watch your Dalmatian slow down, you will know that your time with your sweet pup is coming to an end. Most working dogs tend to suddenly decline, making it very obvious when you need to start taking extra care of their aging bodies. They have trouble on smoother surfaces or can't walk nearly as far as they once did. When it starts to happen, you know to begin to prepare to say goodbye.

Some dogs can continue to live for years after they begin to slow down, but most working dogs don't make it more than a year or two. Sometimes dogs will lose their interest in eating, will have a stroke, or other problems will arise with little warning. Eventually, it will be time to say goodbye, whether at home or at the vet's office. You need to be prepared, and that is exactly why you should be making the most of these last few years.

Talk to your family about how you will care for your dog over the last few years or months of his life. Many dogs will be perfectly happy, despite their limited abilities. Some may begin to have problems controlling their bowel movements, while others may have problems getting up from a prone position. There are solutions to all of these problems. It is key to remember that quality of life should be the primary consideration, and since your dog cannot tell you how he feels, you will have to take cues from your dog. If your dog still seems happy, there is no reason to euthanize him.

At this stage, your dog is probably perfectly happy just sleeping near you for 18 hours a day. That is fine as long as he still gets excited about walking, eating, and being petted. The purpose of euthanasia is to reduce suffering, not to make things more convenient for yourself. This is what makes the decision so difficult, but your dog's behavior should be a fairly good indicator of how he is feeling. Here are some other things to watch to help you evaluate your dog's quality of life:

- Appetite
- Drinking
- Urinating and defecation
- Pain (noted by excessive panting)
- Stress levels

- Desire to be active or with family (If your dog wants to be alone most of the time, that is usually a sign that he is trying to be alone for the end.)

Talk to your vet if your dog has a serious illness to determine what the best path forward is. They can provide the best information on the quality of your dog's life and how long your dog is likely to live with the ailment.

If your dog gets to the point when you know that he is no longer happy, he can't move around, or he has a fatal illness, it is probably time to say goodbye. This is a decision that should be made as a family, always putting the dog's needs and quality of life first. If you decide it is time to say goodbye, determine who will be present at the end.

Once at the vet's office, if you have decided on euthanasia, you can make the last few minutes very happy by feeding your dog the things he couldn't eat before. Things like chocolate and grapes can put a smile on his face for the remaining time he has.

You can also have your dog euthanized at home. If you decide to request a vet to come to your home, be prepared for additional charges. You also need to determine where you want your dog to be, whether inside or outside, and in which room if you decide to do it inside.

Make sure at least one person is present so that your dog is not alone during the last few minutes of his life. You don't want your dog to die surrounded by strangers. The process is fairly peaceful, but your dog will probably be a little stressed. He will pass within a few minutes of the injection. Continue to talk to him as his brain will continue to work even after his eyes close.

Once your dog is gone, you need to determine what to do with the body.

- Cremation is one of the most common ways of taking care of your pet's body. You can get an urn or request a container to scatter your dog's ashes over his favorite places. Make sure you don't dump his ashes in places where that is not permitted. Private cremation is more expensive than communal cremation, but it means that the only ashes you get are from your dog. Communal creation occurs when several pets are cremated together.
- Burial is the easiest method if you have your pet euthanized at home, but you need to check your local regulations to ensure that you can

bury your dog at home, as this is illegal in some places. You also need to consider the soil. If your yard is rocky or sandy, that will create problems. Also, don't bury your pet in your yard if it is near wells that people use as a drinking source or if it is near wetlands or waterways. Your dog's body can contaminate the water as it decays. You can also look into a pet cemetery if there is one in your area.

Grief and Healing

Dogs become members of our families, so their passing can be incredibly difficult. People go through all of the same emotions and feelings of loss with a dog as they do with close friends and family. The absence of that presence in your life is jarring, especially with such a loving, loyal dog like the Dalmatian. Your home is a constant reminder of the loss, and in the beginning, you and your family will probably feel considerable grief. Saying goodbye is going to be difficult. Taking a couple of days off work is not a bad idea. While people who don't have dogs will say that your Dalmatian was just a dog, you know better, and it is okay to feel the pain and to grieve as you would for any lost loved one.

Losing your Dalmatian is also going to make a substantial change in your schedule. It will likely take a while to get accustomed to the way your schedule has shifted. Fight the urge to go out and get a new dog because you almost certainly are not ready yet.

Everyone grieves differently, so you will need to allow yourself to grieve in a way that is healthy for you. Everyone in your family will feel the loss differently, too. Some people don't require much time, while others can feel the loss for months. There is no timetable, so you can't try to force it on yourself or any member of your family.

Talk about how you would like to remember your pup. You can have a memorial for your lost pet, tell stories, or plant a tree in your dog's memory. If someone doesn't want to participate, that is fine.

Try to return to your normal routine as much as possible if you have other pets. This can be both painful and helpful as your other pets will still need you just as much (especially other dogs who have also lost their companion).

If you find that grief is hindering your ability to function normally, seek professional help. If needed, you can go online to find support groups in your area to help you and your family, especially if this was your first dog. Sometimes it helps to talk about the loss so that you can start to heal.

Printed in Great Britain
by Amazon

41752946R00149